ORIGAMI FLOWERS

James Minoru Sakoda

DOVER PUBLICATIONS, INC.
Mineola, New York

Published in Canada by General Publishing Company, Ltd., 30 Lesmill Road, Don Mills, Toronto, Ontario.

Bibliographical Note

Origami Flowers, first published by Dover Publications, Inc., in 1999, is a revised edition of the work originally published by James M. Sakoda in 1992 under the title *Origami Flower Arrangement.*

Library of Congress Cataloging-in-Publication Data

Sakoda, James Minoru, 1916–
    Origami flowers / James Minoru Sakoda.
        p.   cm.
    ISBN 0-486-40285-1 (pbk.)
    1. Origami.   2. Flowers in art.   3. Flower arrangement, Japanese.
I. Title.
TT870.S274   1999
736'.982—dc21   98-27754
                                                                    CIP

Manufactured in the United States of America
Dover Publications, Inc., 31 East 2nd Street, Mineola, N.Y. 11501

Preface

Origami Flower Arrangement is an attempt to set up an all-origami procedure for making flower arrangements--without tapes or wires to secure stems and leaves, *kenzan* or frog for holding the base of stems and all made of foil paper or poster board. Stems are folded as tubes initially and a hole left at one end before being rolled into a tight stem. The hole in the stem is used to connect leaves, flowers and other stems. Vases are folded from poster boards, and have grooves around the bottom edge to hold ends of stems, while the top is closed except through a hole in the center and slots to the corners, thus holding the stem of flowers securely in place. The only concession made to non-origami aid is the use of a small amount of poster putty on the ends of stems to keep them from accidentally falling out from holes or grooves. Another method of strengthening the connection involving stems and leaves is to squeeze the connection and then give it a twist.

Another feature of the book is an attempt to teach the basics of Japanese style flower arrangement, which fortunately features natural growing appearance rather than the formation of bouquet of many flowers grouped close together. The emphasis is upon using three main branches of different heights arranged in different combinations, allowing for attractive displays often based on no more than 3, 5 or 7 flowers. Instead of only showing off the blossoms, the curvature of the stems and the presence of the leaves play an important part. While origami is greatly limited in the ability to produce a large variety of flowers or leaves, the flexibility of shortening or lengthening stems and the ability to twist stems, leaves and flowers in the desired direction make it easier to achieve desired positions than one can working with real plants.

In the second edition published by Dover Publications changes have been made in Chapter 8 through 10. In Chapter 8 the bird base rose and tulip have been introduced as easy to fold but attractive flowers. In Chapter 9 the hexagon vase has been added to the original square one. A base has been added to the bottom of the vase, making it more stable and permits the vase to be tall if desired. In Chapter 9 the width of the paper for stems have been increased to provide adequate strength. Also, both small leaves and tall leaves for bulb flower have been added. In general these changes overcome weaknesses in the folding procedure and provide for greater flexibility.

Poster boards are available in the stationery section of many stores. Poster putty can be found in CVS drugstores. Medium weight foil paper in dull shades are recommended for stems, leaves and flowers. Origami USA in New York City carries supplies of foil paper in 6 inch and 10 inch squares. Instructions in the book are based on using 10 inch squares.

For larger size paper it is usually necessary to buy and cut foil paper in rolls. For my own use I usually buy them from Alufoil Products Co., Inc. at 135 Oser Avenue, Hauppauge, N.Y. 11788. They stock plain foil paper in medium weight (30 lb.) which is suitable for flower arrangement work. Embossing, which makes foil paper more flexible are generally not stocked but can be ordered. When cutting foil paper bought in rolls for flower arrangement and other projects, I prefer to cut paper to a 10 x 12.5 inch size. A mailing manila envelope measuring 12 x 15.5 inches is available for storage or mailing. From the sheets one can cut one 10 inch square or two 6.25 inch squares for most folding. To cover poster boards for vases of varying sizes one can cut two 6.25 x 10 inch or 5 x 12.5 inch rectangles, or one 7-10 inch x 12.5 inch rectangles.. There is a certain amount of wastage and the need to cut to size each time, but it avoids the cost of cutting, collating and storing papers of different sizes.

Table of Contents

Table of Contents

The Wheat Stalk

Chapter 1   A Bit of History

Early Flowers

Flowers have never been very popular in traditional origami and still play a minor part of the repertoire of many expert folders. The traditional bases generally have not lent themselves to folding attractive flowers. A flower made from a bird base has only four petals which are too long and are better suited for a star or wings for birds. The frog base, which is more difficult to fold, provides a more suitable foundation for a flower, and produces the four petal lily or iris with four short points in the center. As I will show later these short points can be changed into white squares to provide a white center cluster. Another base for a traditional flower, the water lily, is the triple blintz fold which involves folding in the corners to the center three times and produces twelve points. The points folded in the back side need to be brought to the front, but unless the paper is strong and soft the move is likely to tear the paper. The square petals also need additional work to make them into attractive petals.

Later Flowers

It is only when one gets into innovative works does one find more attractive flowers. The best source for flowers is Toshie Takahama's flower book, *Hana no Origami* (**Flower Origami**, undated, Yuki Shobo, Tokyo) and *Kurashi o Kazaru Origami* (**Origami to Decorate One's Life, 1969,** Makosha, Tokyo). Her style contrasts with mine in that she, like many other Japanese folders, is more liberal about cutting, adding pieces to make the center of the flower or to add layers of petals and to avoid difficult folds. She names her flowers and makes an effort to match them with appropriate leaves. From time to time in Nippon Origami Association's monthly magazine, *Origami*, there are instructions and displays of origami flowers. In the April, 1990 and October, 1990 issues of *Origami* are instructions and displays of mass of flowers in a basket and others arranged beautifully on paper and framed as a picture. These are by Keiji Kitamura. I have also seen a couple of efforts to show the lovely form of the rose, a challenge to any folder. There is one in the February, 1992 issue by Akiko Yamanishi. In **Top Origami** by Toshie Takahama and Kunihiko Kasahara, (1985, Sanrio Company, Tokyo) there is a beautiful rose by Toshikazu Kawasaki.

The Origami Scene

A relatively easy method of displaying folded flowers is to arrange flowers, folded stems and leaves on paper or cardboard to make a framed picture. This approach to origami display was developed by Mrs. Kyo Araki of Kyoto and reported in her *Kyo-Origami* , (1973, Koseisya-Koseikaku, Tokyo). Among the scenes of Kyoto, there are people, including colorful dancing girls, temples, trees and also flowers and plants. The origami scene has become a popular method of displaying origami and very elaborate pictures are shown at exhibits. The advantage of the flat picture is that it is a relatively simple matter to fold a stem and leaves from narrow strips of paper and connect them to each other and to flowers by pasting them to a sheet of paper or cardboard. A limitation is that everything needs to be folded flat.

Display in a Vase

A more difficult approach is to provide an upright stem to which folded flowers and leaves are attached and the stem placed in some kind of vase. This method is desirable for flowers which are three-dimensional in nature. A common technique to accomplish this is to use artificial flower making methods, which are well known. A stiff wire is used as a stem and green tape is used to attach leaves to the stem as well as to wrap the wire to give it body. The wire can be inserted into the bottom of the flower if there is a hole or a slit. Mrs. Takahama, who used this method trimmed the end of the lily to provide a hole for the stem to enter. The green tape served to hold the flower firmly to the wire stem. This solved the problem of holding the flower upright in a vase as was done with real, imitation or dried flowers.

The objection to the use of wire and tape, of course, was that they were not made of paper. A second approach to making a stem, which used an ancient household technique, was to take a narrow strip of paper and roll it diagonally into a twine called *Koyori*. The flowers and leaves were attached to it with paste. This method was used by Yoshihide and Sumiko Momotani in *Origami, Imeji to Sosaku* (1975, Sogensha, Tokyo).

The Origami Stem

Perhaps the most ambitious attempt to attach flowers and leaves to a stem of folded paper using folding techniques only was made by David Collier (See Eric Kenneway's **Complete Origami**, 1987, St. Martin Press, New York City). Westerners, more often than Japanese, are likely to be purists about allowing cutting and pasting. A square sheet (about six inches?) was cut into fourths, one was discarded, one was cut in half to make a stem and two leaves. Two leaves were first folded and then folded into a narrowed stem. The two longer strips were overlapped to form a longer strip and the sides folded to the center and then the stem with leaves inserted and a second fold made to the center. The net result was a narrow stem about twice the length of the original paper with a

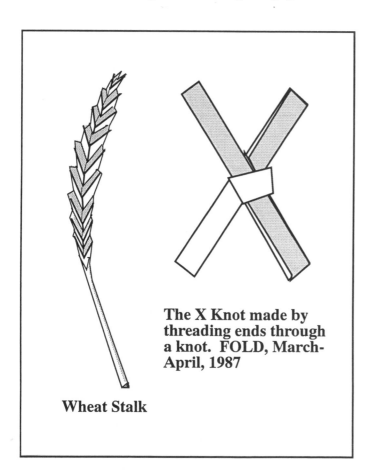

The X Knot made by threading ends through a knot. FOLD, March-April, 1987

Wheat Stalk

stem with leaves attached. The top end of the stem was then inserted into the bottom of the flower, which had a convenient hole underneath. The net result was a flat stem about 5/16 of an inch wide with leaves and flowers, not unlike the stem of the wheat stalk that I made when I worked with knot origami.

The difficulty with the flat stem, as I found, was that it could not be bent easily in all directions, but that it bent too easily into the flat side in spite of attempts to keep it straight. A triangular tube would have been stronger, but then it would be difficult to bend in any direction.

Knot Origami and the Wheat Stalk

My interest in knot origami was aroused by Trish Troy Truitt's writing about it in FOLD, an origami apa or newsletter circulated among about twenty or so subscribers. I first wrote about it in the November-December, 1986 issue and continued to write about it in the April, 1987 issue. Knot origami, which might also be called ribbon origami, consisted of taking a long strip of paper about an inch or so wide and folding it to create both geometric and non-geometric figures. The standard width that I adopted was one inch with the length extending to three or four feet. I started with bond paper, which I initially glued together, but soon shifted to foil paper, which I cut in one long piece from a roll. The paper was originally folded lengthwise in half, the sides folded into the center line, and the whole folded in half again.

This left the paper about a quarter of an inch wide. A key operation of knot origami was usually a series of knots, which form pentagons, with two ends emanating at different angles. By inserting the ends back into the knot, it was possible to get spokes to form a wheel. A series of knots with two spokes could be used to form a series of legs. It was not difficult to form a head by folding a knot at the end of a stem. I made a number of weird creations, but the two that I wrote up in FOLD was the Dodecahedron and the Gion Dancer.

As far as flower arrangement was concerned an important creation was the wheat stalk, which was made by making V-shaped accordion pleats on five or six inches of the end of the strip. In order to make precise accordion pleats the strip was wrapped around itself at a 45 degree angle to get mountain folds equally spaced apart. The stem was cut to a length of 12 or 15 inches, and narrowed down to one-eighth of an inch in width. It was too weak to hold up for long, and easily bent.

Pipe or Tube Origami

My interest in what I called pipe origami came about when Rachel Katz diagrammed a Christmas boot in the November-December, 1990 issue of FOLD. The boot was made of a kite form, with the top rolled down to form the rim for the top of the boot. It was then folded in half and the lower half bent forward using a crimp or double inside reverse fold, which I refer to as a foot fold. She showed how she had improved the boot by pulling out one of the folded in flaps and bringing it on the outside to close the back. I wondered whether it was possible to close the bottom of the boot and also make the boot three dimensional. In the January-February issue I showed how this could be done by pulling out both flaps and overlapping them along the back and bottom. The advantage of the three dimensional boot was the wider opening to hold presents.

This led me to wonder about how to go about bending a triangular tube made by folding a strip of paper into fourths and then overlapping the two end flaps. I worked with $8^1/2$ x 11 inch neon bond paper cut into quarter strips (slightly wider than two inches). I concluded that the easiest way to fold a three dimensional piece was to first fold it in two dimensional form using a crimp or foot fold and then pull out the folded in piece to make the structure three dimensional. This was the same procedure that I had used for the Christmas boot. I found it advantageous to make the bends off center so that loose ends could be tucked into the corners. To use the pipe analogy, the bend gave me an elbow, which allowed for a 90 degree turn. A straight triangular tube could be inserted into an elbow piece. I managed to fold an elbow with a hole at the bend into which it was possible to insert another pipe to form a T. I also learned to make 120 degree bends. By connecting pieces together it was possible to make some structures rising on two or three legs, as well as a dodecahedron. The most useful object that I made was the square chain link, made by making four bends and inserting one end into the other. Several links in different colors could be intertwined to make an attractive decorative piece.

The Inserting and Flexible Stem

I tried the wheat stalk using neon bond letter

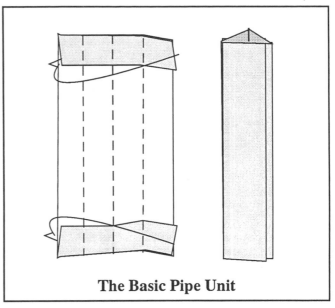

The Basic Pipe Unit

size paper strips about two inches wide and found it to be fairly attractive. It came in five different colors, and among them was an orange, which I liked for the wheat stalk. But I ended up by using all of the five colors. Using about half of an eleven inch length to fold the wheat stalk left about half for a short stem. This was narrowed in half by folding sides into the center line and forming a three sided tube about a quarter of an inch wide on each side. It was a natural step to use another eleven inch strip to fold a stem as a tube into which the stem of the wheat could be inserted. To emphasize the node of the stem, the end piece folded under for the pipe was brought to the outside, and omitted entirely at the other end. An important additional step taken was to leave a hole at one end of the stem and fold the remainder of the stem in half along the side with overlapping edges. This provided flexibility for the stem, which the triangular tube did not have, while retaining much of the strength of the triangular tube. The end was narrowed even more for insertion into the hole of the stem, and this was extended to the entire length of the stem, thus slimming it down to about an eight of an inch and adding to its strength.

The Development of the Leaf

The connection between the wheat stalk and the stem gave me an opportunity to try to create and insert a leaf into the same opening. I took a strip of paper about 1 x 5 inches, folded it diagonally, and then folded the excess inside. I later developed a lock so that the side would not gape open. This added the need to distinguish between right and left side leaves. Thus not only the leaf but a method of attaching it to the stem without tape or glue was found. The leaf did contribute to the attractiveness of the arrangement of wheat stalks in a vase later on.

The Development of the Vase

The tube vase benefited from works of others on boxes. At the last origami convention I had sat in on a class for folding Phillip Shen's fancy hexagonal box, and was therefore aware of the diagonal folds along the corners of the end pieces which allowed the closing of the ends. But the vase also benefited from the work on pipe origami. I was thinking of how it might be possible to avoid the wasted paper when a box is made by putting the bottom in the middle of the paper and bringing up the sides and having to fold in the excess, when the idea of using a tube came to mind. Light letter size cardboard stock was first folded into fifths and then folded into a four-sided tube.

To close one end, half of the width of the side was folded in, diagonal folds made at the corner to complete the bottom of the box. The top of the box was folded in the same way, but in order to have a narrow opening to hold flowers, the ends were folded in along the sides and only half of it was folded out toward the center, forming a dropped and narrowed opening at the top. Some

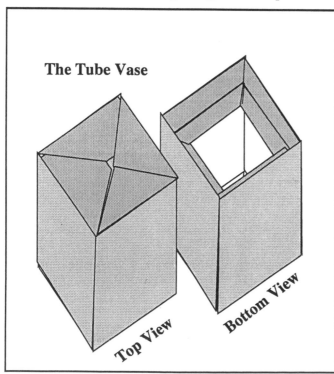

The Tube Vase

Top View

Bottom View

dried flowers were put in the vase and the center opening appeared to work well as I had hoped. But when a large allium with a ball about nine inches across was put in the vase, it tipped over. On a hunch I turned the vase over and put the stem of the allium in the small hole in the center of what was the bottom of the box. And lo and behold the allium and the vase did not tip over. This is how the bottom of the box came to be used as the top, where the center hole and the slit to the corners could be used as vises to hold the stems in place. This solved a problem faced by flower arrangers who often needed to wedge cut stems to hold stems in position.

The problem of tipping was reduced further by using the heavier poster board, which was initially selected because it was available in black, and by making the vase wider and shorter in height. At one point I considered the standard vase size to be made from a poster board measuring 7 x 13 inches and 4.5 inches tall and 2.5 inches along the sides. At the present time the vase is made from 6 x 13 inch poster board, and measures 3.5 inches tall and 2.5 inches wide and is used with stems and leaves cut from 10 inch square paper.

Another fortuitous finding was that the folded-in ends along the insides of the vase could be used to wedge the bottom of the stems. The main danger was bending the stem in attempting to force the stems into the slot, and it was sometimes necessary to make a preliminary hole with the sharp end of a pencil or flat screwdriver before inserting the stem. This feature made it unnecessary to use a *Kenzan* or frog to hold the stems. Thus the vase was ready to use without the need for other accessories often used in flower arrangement.

The Newport Black Ship Festival, 1991

Having folded the wheat stalk, made the stems and leaves and prepared the vase, I planned to teach it at the Black Ship Festival, held annually at Newport, Rhode Island, to commemorate Commodore Perry's opening up of Japan. This was an annual event in which I participated by teaching a couple of classes on origami--mostly to beginners. When I made a sample arrangement of three wheat stalks arranged in a vase and sent it to the Japan America Society to be displayed, it was suggested that it be used as a display for the festival ball, a black tie affair. Knowing very little about flower arrangement I consulted a family friend, Mrs. Yasko Suzuki, who had studied the Sogetsu method of flower arrangement, for a suitable arrangement. She suggested the use of a black vase to set off the orange color, which led me to use poster board in place of light card board. She arranged the two longer wheat stems on one side, hanging down in a similar fashion and the shorter one facing the other direction. As it turned out the poster board was easily folded with the aid of a little pre-creasing. I had to make 20 arrangements, which required time and effort.

This event, however, impressed upon me the fact that origami flower arrangement could have a practical as well as artistic value. It could play a useful part in decorating a home as a centerpiece at a dinner table or as a decoration on a mantel or even a work desk. It tied in directly with the ancient art of flower arrangement which was still taught in Japan. The folding process as well as the flower arrangement could be taught, I thought. All of this was possible with relatively little expenditure for material.

From Wheat Stalks to Flowers

The wheat stalks using neon bond paper was only partially successful. When the arranged wheat stalks were returned, many of them were in poor condition. Some of the flowers and leaves came off, and some of the stalks were bent beyond repair. Part of it was due to the weakness of the paper. It could not be expected to hold up against excessive moisture, for example, or against abuse during transportation and handling. Even before the Black Ship Festival had started I began to experiment with foil paper, and decided that it was definitely stronger than paper. Even so, I felt that doubling the width of the paper would provide more adequate strength. I also began to fold and arrange flowers and asked Mrs. Suzuki to help arrange them.

I borrowed the beginning book on Sogetsu style of flower arrangement called *Sogetsu no Ikebana, Nyumon* (**Beginner's Sogetsu Flower Arrangement** by Hiroshi Teshigahara). The book covered the basics of *Nageire* , involving the use of an upright vase and *Moribana*, which relied on a flat vase. Both English and Japanese texts were provided. I also began to read a book which my wife had purchased long ago called *Ikenobo no Ikebana* by Yuchiku Fujiwara written in Japanese and another **Best of Ikebana, Ikenobo School** by Senei Ikenobo written in English. I felt like an amateur groping for some understanding of the intricacies of Japanese flower arrangement. The initial cutting of stems of three different sizes and arranging them was definite

and clear, but after that the process of filling in and adjusting *(ashirau)* was very vague. Initially I relied on Mrs. Suzuki to do the arrangement for me, but gradually began to develop my own method of arranging the flowers.

Origami Flowers

Over the years I had developed a number of flowers based on the blintzed bird base, which allowed for eight petals. The base of the petals were locked in so that the flower would hold together. The eight petals were expanded to sixteen to make the chrysanthemum. I reviewed the method I had developed to make white center clusters for the lily folded from a frog base, and the rose that I made from the swirl. This effort led to some new flowers, such as the balloon flower. Working with the pentagon and hexagon, which I had previously neglected, expanded the variety of flowers that could be folded. I reviewed Jacques Justin's method of folding a non-square paper into a perfect bird base, which allowed for flowers with varying lengths of petals.

Source of Material

I worried about source of material. Poster boards were available in many places including stationary section of department or discount stores, office supply stores, art supply stores. The preferred color was black, which was usually available. It came in sheets of 22 x 28 inches, and could be easily cut with a paper cutter or a pair of scissors. One of the problems with poster boards was that they did not protect against greasy fingers, for example. I had some light card board stock with foil on both sides, but they turned out to be too light. I then tried gluing silver and gold foil paper on the black poster board, putting Dennison glue stick glue around the edge. This was enough to hold the foil in place, and after folding the combination into a vase, found it beautifully covered with foil. This was at least a temporary solution of the problem.

Foil wrapping paper used to be plentiful at Christmas time, but became scarce, having been replaced by less costly plasticized paper. The problem was not only to get foil paper, but to get the right quality and color and preferably have them cut to the right size for ready use. They generally came in rolls of 15 or 25 feet in length by 26 or 36 inches wide. I had accumulated many rolls of Christmas wrapping paper over the years, but for flowers I decided that the dull pastel shades provided by a foil company in New York was the most suitable. I had first learned of this company from Trish Troy Truitt through FOLD. I had some rolls from a previous order, but in addition ordered some more. I was used to cutting paper for my own use and did not mind it, but I worried about others who would not go to that trouble.

I knew that Friends of the Origami Center, 15 West 77th Street, New York, NY 10024-5192, carried six and ten inch foil paper in a variety of colors. In order to make use of this source of foil paper I decided to change the dimensions of the cut foil paper from $6^1/_2$ by 13 inches to a ten inch square. The instructions for folding stems and leaves were changed to use ten inch square foil paper. The thickness of the foil was relatively heavy and suitable for making strong stems. A property of foil which was attractive was its sheen, which give flowers variation in color depending upon how the light shined on it. However, too much reflection was objectionable, and I preferred the pastel or dull shades. For one thing, they were less likely to crack when they were folded than the brighter shades.

Colors

It was necessary to choose the color of the stem and leaves and the flowers so that they would match. Wheat stalks could be gold, stems could be green or blue green, while paper for flowers were generally selected from among the warm tones--lilac, pink, red, yellow. I use silver paper in place of white. Using the colors available from the source used by the Friends, I decided to recommend the following combinations:

Stems and Leaves	Flowers
Dull Opal	Dull Heliotrope
Dull Opal	Dull Lilac
Dull Opal	Dull Pink
Dull Light Blue	Dull Pink
Dull Nile Green	Dull Lilac
Dull Green	Dull Heliotrope
Dull Green	Dull Yellow
Dull Green	Dull Copper
Dull Green	Dull Lilac

The first choice for stems and leaves was Dull Opal, which was attractive and could be combined with Dull Heliotrope or Dull Lilac or Dull Pink. The second choice for stems and leaves was Dull Green, which could be combined with Dull Heliotrope, Dull Yellow, Dull Copper or

Dull Lilac. I used copper for Chinese lanterns, and substitute for orange and red. I did not order the dull red because it appeared too bright and brittle.

The Need for a Package of Paper

Since foil paper in the desired quality, size and color is not readily available, it would be convenient if someone sold a packet of ten inch foil paper of the desired quality, size and color. The packet might consist of four, six or eight 10-inch sheets each of the following colors: Dull Opal, Dull Opal (double order), Dull Heliotrope, Dull Lilac, Dull Light Blue, Dull Pink, Dull Green, Dull Yellow, Dull Silver, Dull Gold, Dull Copper, Dull Nile Green. To this might be added a dozen black poster boards cut to 6 x 13 inch size and some foil paper, particularly silver and gold cut to the same size as the poster board to cover it. Flowers can be folded from five inch square paper, obtained by cutting a ten inch square paper. But 6 or $6^1/_2$ inch paper, which is commonly used in origami, is also desirable.

The Need for a Textbook

I am planning to teach the folding of a flower or two, the vase, stems and leaves and also how to put them together and make a Japanese style of Ikebana arrangement at the 1992 origami convention in New York City. This, of course, calls for some kind of instruction booklet, and I have decided to use my Macintosh computer and laser printer to do a self publishing job for a few hundred copies of the first edition of a book on making and arranging origami flowers. My task now is to make camera ready copies of the pages. I am using Canvas 3.0, which has many convenient drawing features, to do the drawings. The main difficulty has been doing the freehand three dimensional drawings of the finished product. For the page layout I am using Studio-Design. It provides all of the usual conveniences of allowing for setting up of columns of text which are connected to one another, for chapter headings and automatic page numbers, insertion of drawings from Canvas into designated rectangles on a page, importing of text from a Word 4.0. Pictures of flower arrangements were taken with a camcorder and the use of MacVision 3.0. The printing is to be done by a copy center located near Brown University. The outfit also provides the spiral binding, which allows the pages to open out flat.

Chapter 2　Beginning Lessons on Paper Folding

Start at the beginning

For those who are relatively new to paper folding, it is important to start at the beginning and start to learn the symbols and terms and their meaning. Even for those who are experienced folders it is important to become acquainted with an author's particular set of symbols and terms. Both a table of symbols and an exercise in their use is given at the beginning. An action to be taken is given generally in three ways--dotted lines indicating a valley fold or mountain fold, an arrow showing the direction in which the move is to be made, and verbal written instructions. Every action can be checked by looking at the next drawing. If the action is wrong, then one needs to go back and check the action taken. One way to approach a difficult situation is to make all of the valley and mountain folds indicated and see whether or not things will fall into place.

There are symbols which may be unfamiliar to some folders. The fold and unfold or creasing action is shown by a curve with an arrow at both ends. I find the use of a double curve excessive. The dotted line on the outside crease indicates reversal of a crease from a mountain to a valley fold, and is important in indicating where reverse folds are to be made. The hollow arrow is used to indicate insert or pull out and implies the need to open out and reach in. The look and feel of a symbol are important. The push in symbol is a black large arrow. I would suggest going through the exercise a couple of times, which starts with a white square and ends up as a preliminary fold with a sunken center.

Drawings are generally arranged, not left to right, left to right but in a zigzag fashion: left to right, right to left, left to right. A good reason for this is that it is possible to keep the next instruction only one step away, thus making it easier to compare with the previous one. It also makes the arrangement of the drawings more flexible and permits making maximum use of the available space. To make instructions easier to find the numbers have been enlarged.

Square Preliminary Fold and Bird Base

To get to the bird base or the frog base it is necessary to fold the preliminary fold, which I have referred to as the square preliminary fold. As one moves to the use of the pentagon, hexagon or free form folding the term square becomes inaccurate and probably should be dropped. The term square preliminary fold is useful because there is a triangular counterpart to the square one, which is the one used for the water bomb. But that base is generally referred to as the water bomb base.

Some Easy Flowers

The water lily made from a bird base is taken from my **Modern Origami** . The water bomb or balloon is traditional--i.e. it has existed for many years--and is included here because it can be used as a Chinese lantern. It can be folded in red or copper. The lily or iris made from a frog base is traditional and is the best known among origami flowers.

Lily with a White Center Cluster

The first new entry into newer types of flower folding is the lily with a cluster of four white squares. It is provided with a hole at the bottom by sinking the center point. If this is too much trouble at this point it is possible, as Mrs. Toshie Takahama does, to snip off the end to make a hole. The folding procedure for the little squares is a bit troublesome, but the square clusters appear at the end as if by magic. Once the procedure is learned it can be applied to the frog base made from a pentagon or hexagon.

On to flower arrangement

Once some flowers are folded, it is possible to go on to the chapter on vase, stems and leaves and then to the last chapter on flower arrangement.

Origami Symbols

Name	Symbol
Turn over	
Fold in front	
Valley fold	— — — — —
Fold behind	
Mountain fold	— ∙ — ∙ — ∙ —
Fold then unfold (Crease)	
Rotate	
Insert or pull out	
Enlarge	
Push in	
Xray Eye	∙ ∙ ∙ ∙ ∙ ∙ ∙ ∙

Exercise

Before Action	After Action

Uncolored side up → Colored side up

Diagonal valley fold   Unfold   Diagonal crease

Mountain fold   Fold, unfold (Precrease)   Rotate

Inside reverse fold   Repeat   Square Preliminary Fold

Precrease   Sink the center point by opening flat and mountain folding creases.   Sink completed

The Square Preliminary Fold

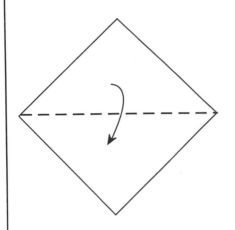

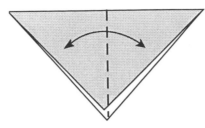

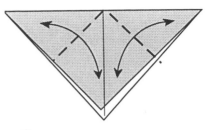

2. Precrease down the center line.

3. Precrease on each side by folding the folded edge to the center line and unfolding.

1. Start with a square with the uncolored side up. Make a diagonal valley fold.

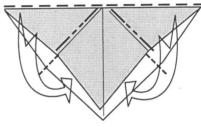

5. The Square Preliminary Fold.

4. Inside reverse fold the folded edges on both sides into the center line.

The Bird Base

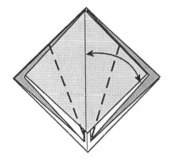

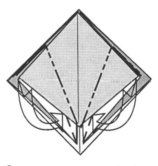

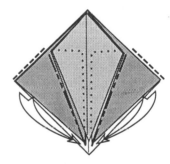

1. Start with the **Square Preliminary Fold.** Precrease by folding the raw edges on both sides to the center line and unfolding.

2. Inside reverse fold the raw edges to the center line.

3. Repeat the inside reverse folds on the back.

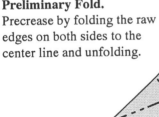

5. Creases of the bird base.

4. The Bird Base

The Bird Base Water Lily

Published in **Modern Origami** by James M. Sakoda, 1969, Simon and Schuster, New York, N.Y.

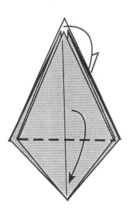

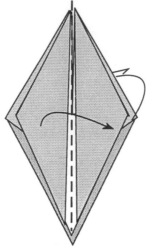

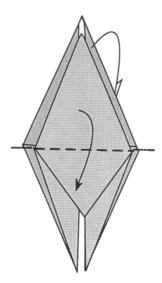

1. Start with the bird base turned upside down from the usual position. Fold down the front and rear flaps at their widest point.

2. Book fold (like turning pages) the front and rear flaps to get at the side ones.

3. Fold down the front and rear flaps once again.

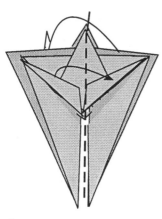

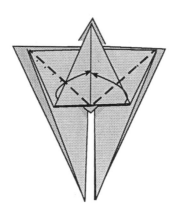

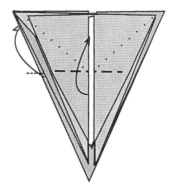

5. Cover the folded flap with a fold of the two lower corners. Repeat behind.

4. Fold up the front and rear flaps at the base of the inverted triangle.

6. Book fold the front and back and repeat Steps 4 and 5 on the remaining two flaps.

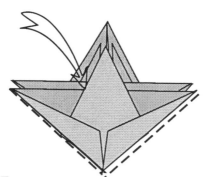

7. Open out the four petals.

8. The Bird Base Water Lily.

Frog Base Lily, Traditional

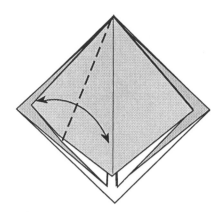

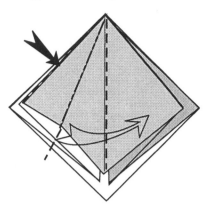

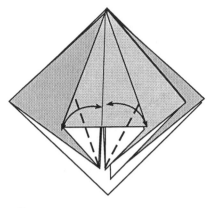

1. Start with the Square Preliminary Fold. Precrease one flap by folding the folded edge to the center line.

2. Squash Fold. Open out the inside of the flap and push down on the mountain folded ridge.

3. Precrease the lower sides by folding the raw edges to the center line.

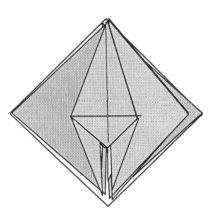

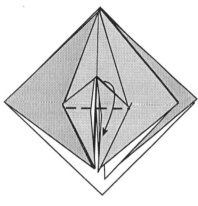

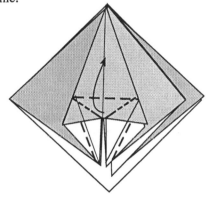

6. Complete Steps 1 - 5 for the remaining three flaps.

5. For the frog the short flap is tucked under, but for the flower let it be folded down outside.

4. With your fingernail make a crease connecting the ends of two creases. Then pull up the short flap and fold in the sides.

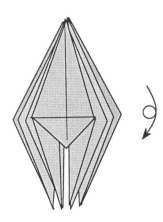

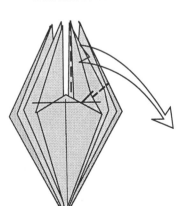

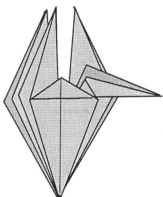

7. The Frog Base. Flip upside down.

8. Inside reverse fold one petal into a horizontal position.

9. Repeat Step 8 on the remaining three flaps. Then open out the petals. The lily is also folded as the Iris.

10. The Frog Base Lily.

Waterbomb-Chinese Lantern

The traditional waterbomb (balloon to the Japanese) can be used as a Chinese Lantern. Use orange or copper paper.

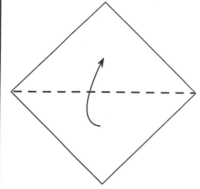

1. Start with a square, uncolored side up. Fold up the lower corner.

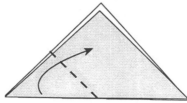

2. Valley fold the left corner to the top.

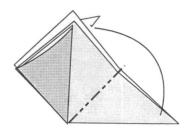

3. Mountain fold the right corner to the top. (Turn the paper over and do a valley fold.)

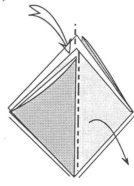

4. Open out the inside and squash flat to one side. Rotate so that the peak is on top.

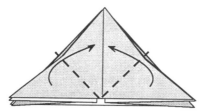

5. The Triangular Waterbomb Base. Fold sides in along the center line.

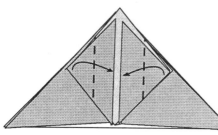

6. Fold the side corners of the folded flaps into the midpoint of the center line.

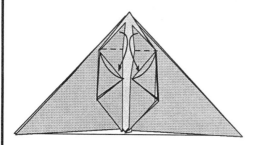

7. Fold the two short flaps down in half.

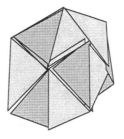

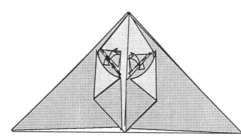

8. Open out the pocket by pulling back the short flap toward the center line and fold the short flap in so that it is inserted in the pocket. Repeat on the other side. Then repeat Steps 5-8 on the back.

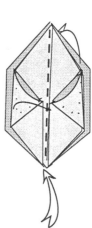

9. Spread out the four flaps and then blow into the hole below.

10. The Water Bomb-Chinese Lantern. Note the vertical valley fold creases.

Lily with a White Center

The traditional lily can be provided with an attractive white center. In addition the base is sunk to provide a hole for a stem.

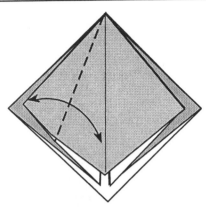

1. Start with the Square Preliminary Fold. Precrease one flap by folding the folded edge to the center line.

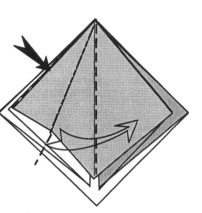

2. Squash Fold. Open out the inside of the flap and push down on the mountain folded ridge.

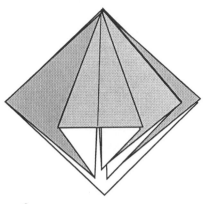

3. Repeat the squash fold on the remaining three flaps.

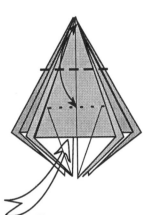

5. Precrease the point down to the level of the upper ends of the creases. Then open out to a square.

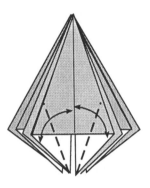

4. Precrease by folding the lower raw edges to the center line. Unfold.

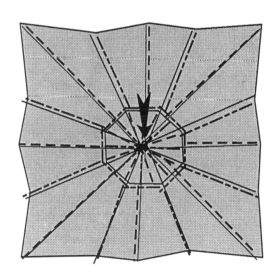

6. Sinking the center point. Mountain fold along edges of the center octagon. Then push in the center and accordion pleat the outside and inside of the octagon until the entire piece is flattened down neatly.

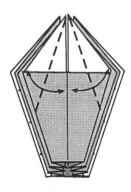

7. Precrease by folding and unfolding the raw edges to the center line.

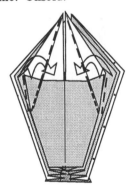

8. Inside reverse fold. Fold in the raw edges under the flap in front only up to the preliminary crease line (This is different from the frog base operation which goes beyond it.)

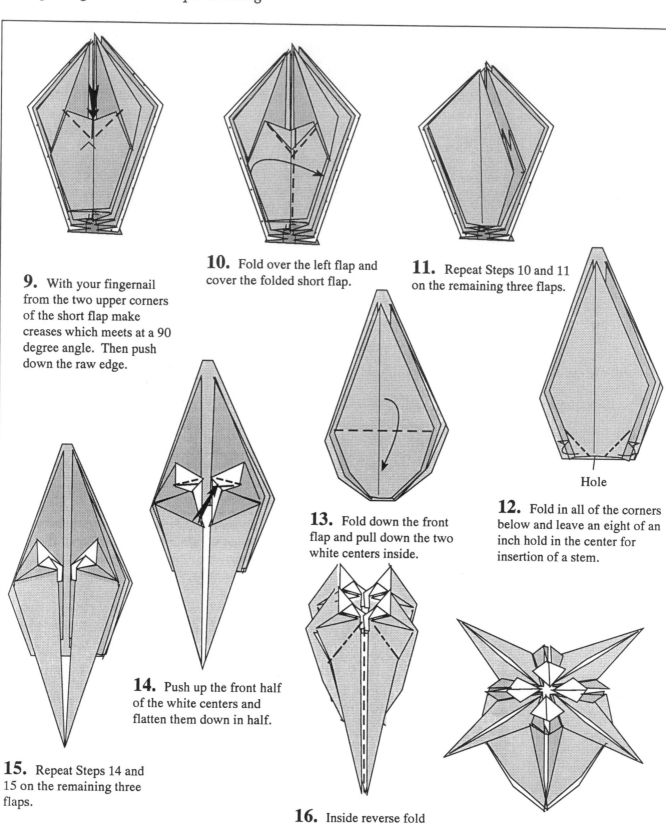

9. With your fingernail from the two upper corners of the short flap make creases which meets at a 90 degree angle. Then push down the raw edge.

10. Fold over the left flap and cover the folded short flap.

11. Repeat Steps 10 and 11 on the remaining three flaps.

Hole

12. Fold in all of the corners below and leave an eight of an inch hold in the center for insertion of a stem.

13. Fold down the front flap and pull down the two white centers inside.

14. Push up the front half of the white centers and flatten them down in half.

15. Repeat Steps 14 and 15 on the remaining three flaps.

16. Inside reverse fold the four flaps into a horizontal position and open out into petals.

17. Lily with a White Center.

Chapter 3 PENTAGON AND HEXA-GON FLOWERS

Important Bases Ignored

Origami generally begins with a square piece of paper. To get more points it is convenient to simply fold the corners into the center and fold the familiar bird or frog bases. As a result I have always thought of the blintzed bird base as the flower base and have rarely used the pentagon or the hexagon. In Modern Origami I even used the center point of the frog base to make the five petals for the cherry blossom, a difficult task because of the many layers of paper involved. This time I used the pentagon to fold the frog base and from it the cherry blossom with clusters of little white squares in the center. I have found the pentagon bird and frog bases to be extremely versatile for flower folding and believe that they should be frequently used.

The hexagon is very close to the pentagon in form and anything folded with the pentagon can be folded using a hexagon paper. The main difference is that the petals are shorter and wider proportionately. I have not bothered to write separate instructions for the hexagon, but some flowers, such as daffodils, for example, may look more natural with six rather than five petals. The folding with a hexagon is easier than using the blintzed bird base.

Cutting the Pentagon and Hexagon

Cutting the square into a pentagon or hexagon is not difficult. Both methods given here are mathematically accurate. The method of cutting the pentagon I owe to Koji and Mitsuye Husimi's *Origami no Kikagaku* (The Geometry of Origami). I am not sure where I learned the cutting of the hexagon. It is consistent with the well known method of folding an equal lateral triangle by folding sides to the center line so that all three sides are equal in length.

Method of Folding the Pentagon

One of the consequence of changing the number of petals from four to five or six is that the method of folding needs to be changed a little. I find it easier to use the pre-ceasing method of making valley folds to the corners and mountain folds to the sides than the usual method of reverse folds. For one thing, the same instruction can be applied to four, five or six sided paper. Another difference is the extent to which the center point is sunk.

The Pentagon Bird Base Flowers

The impatiens illustrates how petals can be shortened and made to lie flat and overlap one another. The cherry blossom has five notched petals, a requirement which can be met by notching the edges of the petals from a flower folded from a pentagon. In this chapter the cherry blossom is provided with a white center by fully sinking the bird base and countersinking 1/3 of the center point. The notching procedure is the one used in Modern Origami.

The Daffodil with a White Center

The procedure for the cherry blossom with the white center can be modified to fold a daffodil with a white center cup. The procedure is to start with a hexagon and fully sink the inner hexagon, but countersink only about a quarter of the center in order to form the cup.

Five Petal Balloon Flower

The balloon flower is new. The bird base is modified by using a somewhat complicated sinking of the corners. An attractive feature is that it has both an open and closed positions. It can also pass for a tulip.

The Pentagon Frog Base Flowers

The frog base for the pentagon and hexagon are needed largely to take advantage of the short flaps for the iris and the cherry blossom's white cluster. A daffodil was added.

Cutting the Pentagon

These directions for accurately cutting a pentagon from a square were borrowed from Koji and Mitsuye Fushimi's ***Origami no Kikagaku*** (The Geometry of Origami), 1979, Tokyo, Nippon Hyoronsha).

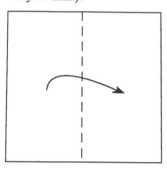

1. Take a square sheet and fold in half vertically.

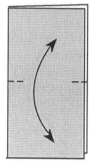

2. Fold in half and make creases on both sides.

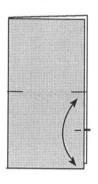

3. Fold the lower righthand corner to the crease line and leave a crease.

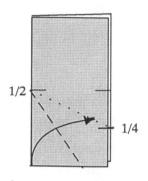

4. Fold or imagine a line from the left halfway point to the right quarter point. and fold the folded edge to that line.

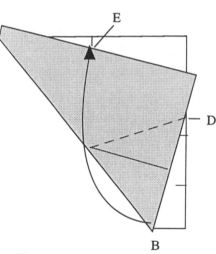

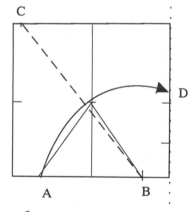

6. Fold B-C so that A touches the right edge of the square. This point is labeled D.

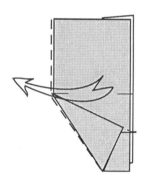

5. Open out to a square.

7. Fold Point B so that it ends up on the raw edge in line with the center vertical crease. The crease line should also end at D.

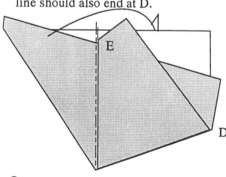

8. Fold under the left side along the vertical center line.

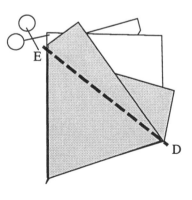

9. Make a straight cut from E to D.

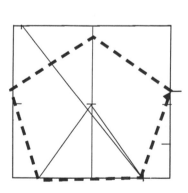

10. The cutout Pentagon.

Cutting the Hexagon

The hexagon, with six sides, can be folded in the same way as the pentagon with five with very little change except for proportions. The cutting of the hexagon and the folding of the preliminary fold is shown here.

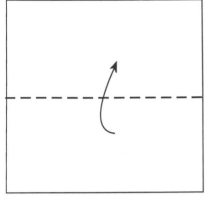

1. Start with a square with the uncolored side up. Fold horizontally in half.

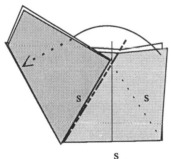

2. Fold vertically in half and unfold.

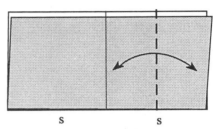

3. Fold one side to the center line and unfold.

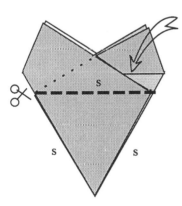

4. Start a fold at the base of the center line and fold the lower left corner to the one quarter line on the right.

6. Make a straight cut from one corner to the other. Then open out flat.

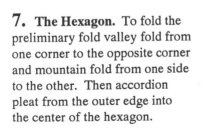

5. Mountain fold the right side along the folded edge. The corner should just reach the folded edge on the other side.

7. The Hexagon. To fold the preliminary fold valley fold from one corner to the opposite corner and mountain fold from one side to the other. Then accordion pleat from the outer edge into the center of the hexagon.

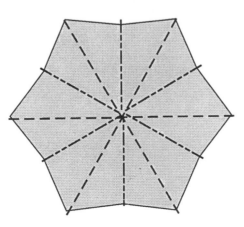

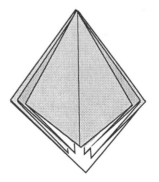

8. The Hexagon Preliminary Fold. Try pentagon routines on it.

Pentagon Bird Base

Many of the flowers folded from a square can also be folded from a pentagon to form flowers with five petals. The petals are shorter and wider so that in place of the full sinking of the center square it is only have sunk.

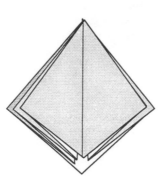

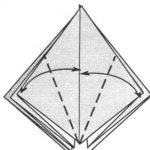

2. The Preliminary Fold. Choose the bird base or the frog base. The frog base is generally more useful.

3. Fold raw edges to the center line and unfold.

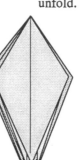

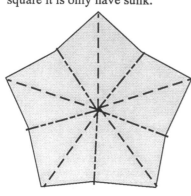

1. Start with a pentagon. Valley fold from the center to the corners and mountain fold to the sides. Then accordion pleat into the preliminary fold (no longer square).

4. Inside reverse fold all flaps into the center line.

5. The Pentagon Bird Base.

Impatiens

Some flowers, such as the Impatiens, have rounded or notched tips, unlike many flowers which end in points. The petals are also wide and overlap one another. This effect can be obtained with a five petal flower base.

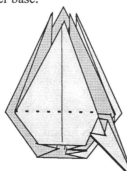

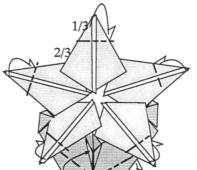

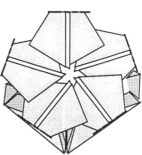

1. Start with the half sunk pentagon bird base. Modify the usual petal folding by accordion pleating the base.

2. Complete the petal folding for the remaining four flaps. Then open out the petals flat and allow them to overlap one another.

3. Mountain fold about 1/3 of the ends of the petals. Then fold the corners at the bottom to form a narrow hole to hold stems.

4. Impatiens. If desired notch the ends of the petals, using the technique for the cherry blossom.

Five Petal Flowers

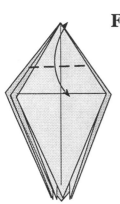

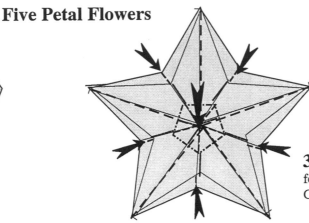

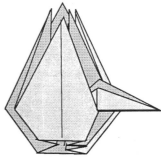

1. Start with the Pentagon Bird Base. Fold the top center down to the crease line and unfold the center section.

2. Sinking the Center Point. Mountain fold the inner pentagon and push down the center. At the same time accordion pleat the outer edges into their original positions.

3. Fold down the front flap and then fold a petal into a horizontal position. Cover with the adjoining flap.

4. Complete the petals for the remaining four flaps. Then open them out.

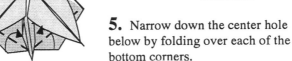

5. Narrow down the center hole below by folding over each of the bottom corners.

6. The Basic Five Petal Flower.

Cherry Blossom

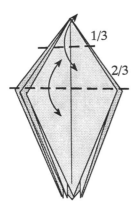

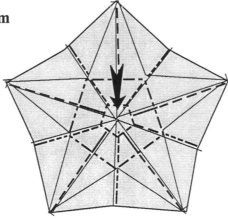

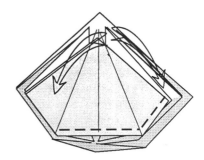

1/3

2/3

6. Start with the pentagon bird base. Make preliminary creases at the widest point and a point 1/3 from the top. Then open out to a square.

7. Mountain fold the larger pentagon. Then push down on the center to sink the point. Accordion pleat the outer edges as shown. Countersink the smaller pentagon--- i.e. push up from below.

8. Open out two adjacent flaps

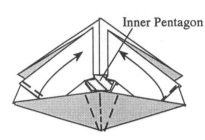

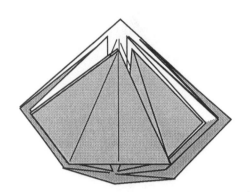

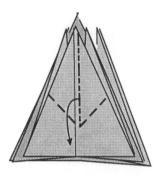

4. Lay the center of the lower flap on the ridge of the inner smaller pentagon and fold in the two sides into their original positions.

5. Repeat Steps 8 and 9 on the remaining four flaps.

6. Fold a petal starting where the paper is caught.

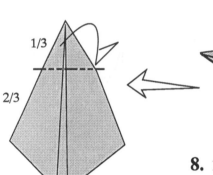

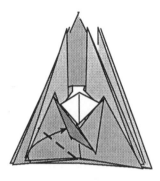

9. Notching the Petal. Fold down 1/3 of the end of a petal and mountain fold under.

8. Five Petal Flower with a White Center. For a cherry blossom notch the ends of the petals.

7. Complete the petals for the remaining four flaps. Then fold up the bottom corners to narrow the center hole to hold a stem.

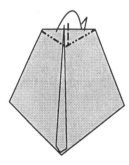

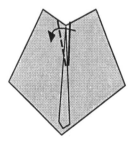

10. Make a triangular mountain fold to form a notch at the end of the petal.

11. Accordion pleat the middle of the notch to allow it to fold flat.

12. The Cherry Blossom.

Five Petal Balloon Flower

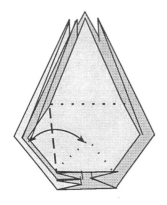

1. Start with the **half sunk pentagon bird base**. Make a preliminary crease so that half of the length of the petal is folded in.

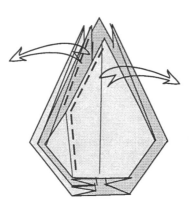

2. Open out the two petals on both sides of the crease.

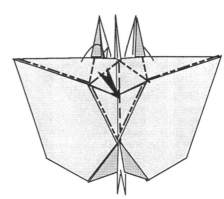

3. Sinking the corner. Make a V-shaped mountain fold at the top of the flap and push in the center and bring the two sides together.

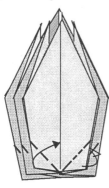

6. Fold the bottom corners to narrow the center hold to hold a stem.

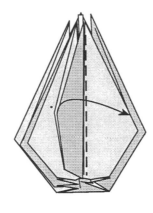

5. Fold over the flap which had its corner sunk. Repeat Steps 1-4 on the remaining flaps.

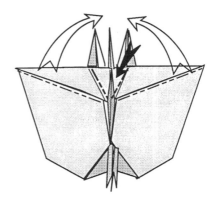

4. Topple the sunken ridge to one side and push down the center edge of the flap all the way in and bring the two flaps together.

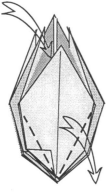

7. Open out the flaps and push out the sides into a bowl shape.

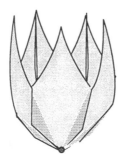

8. The Balloon Flower (Platycodon).

9. Fold the petals in for the unopened balloon position.

Pentagon Frog Base

Many of the flowers folded from a square can also be folded from a pentagon to create flowers with five petals. These are shorter and wider than for the square and provide for variation in flower types.

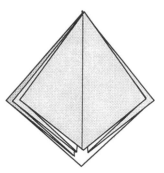

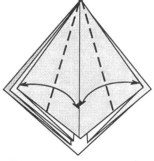

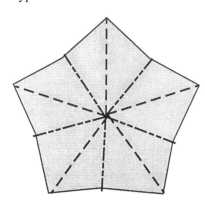

1. Start with a pentagon. Valley fold from the center to the corners and mountain fold to the sides. Then accordion pleat into the preliminary fold (no longer square).

2. The Preliminary Fold. Choose the bird base or the frog base. The frog base is generally more useful.

3. Fold the folded edges into the center line and unfold.

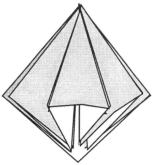

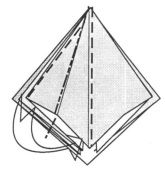

4. Inside reverse fold the folded edge into the center line.

5. Repeat Steps 3 and 4 for the remaining four petals.

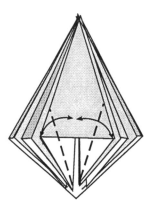

6. The Incomplete Frog Base. Fold in the raw edges of the front flap. Unfold.

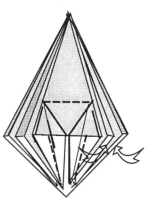

7. Inside reverse fold the raw edge and at the same time form a triangular short flap. Repeat on the remaining four flaps.

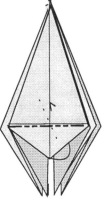

8. Tuck each of the five flaps under.

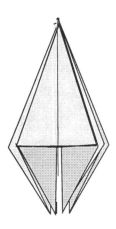

9. The Pentagon Frog Base.

Pentagon Frog Base Iris

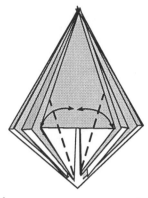

1. Start with the incomplete pentagon frog base. Fold in the lower sides to the center line and unfold.

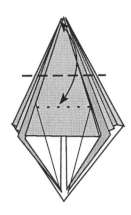

2. Fold the center point down to the top of the crease lines and then unfold the entire sheet out flat.

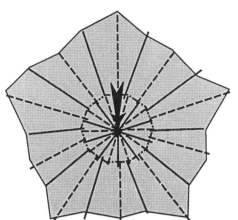

3. Sinking the Center Point. Mountain fold the ten sided polygon and accordion pleat around the edge while pushing down the center point.

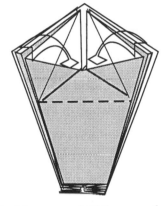

4. Inside reverse fold the raw edges to the center line. Leave the short triangular flap out.

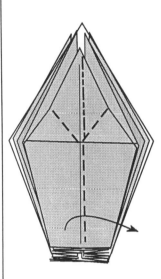

6. Fold a petal and let it stretch out horizontally. Cover with an adjoining flap.

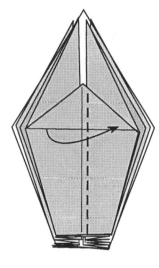

5. Bookfold one flap over to get at the next flap. Then complete the inside reverse folds for the remaining 4 flaps.

7. Complete the folding of the petals. Open out the petals and shape as desired. Fold the bottom corners to narrow the hole for the stem.

8. The Five Petal Iris. To change the short flaps to white clusters use the technique used with the four petal lily.

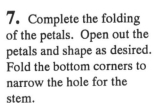

Pentagon Cherry Blossom

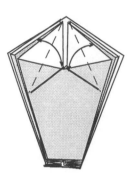

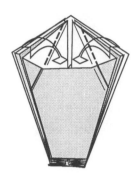

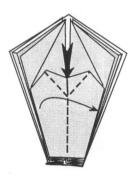

1. Start with the incomplete pentagon frog base with the point sunk (Step 4 of the Pentagon Frog Base Lily). On the top flap fold in upper edges to the center line and unfold.

2. Fold in the raw edges under the flap in front, but only to the preliminary crease line. (This is different from the frog base operation which meet in the center.)

3. With your fingernail make creases from both corners of the front flap which meet at a right angle. Then push down on the upper edge and fold over the left flap to cover the folded short flap.

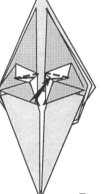

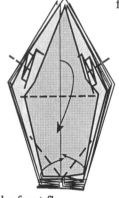

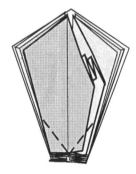

6. The front half of the white center should bend in half. Push up from below if it needs help. Then flatten them down .

5. Pull down the front flap while also pulling down the two white centers underneath.

4. Repeat Steps 1 -3 on the remaining four flaps. Also fold in all of the lower corners.

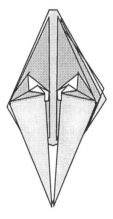

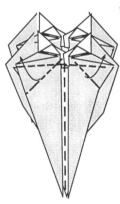

7. Repeat Steps 5 and 6 on the remaining flaps.

8. Lift up each flap and fold a petal in the usual fashion.

9. **Pentagon Flower with a white cluster.**

10. **Pentagon Cherry Blossom.** The petals are notched. See Page 20.

Pentagon Frog Base Daffodil

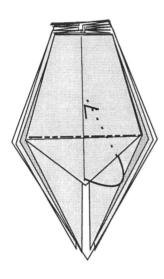

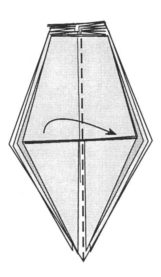

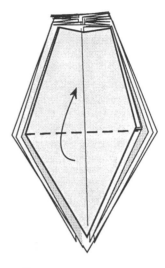

1. Start with the pentagon frog base with the center point sunk about one quarter of its length. (See Step 5 of the Pentagon Frog Base Iris.) Tuck the short flaps under.

2. Flip over one flap to get a single flap.

3. Fold up the flap.

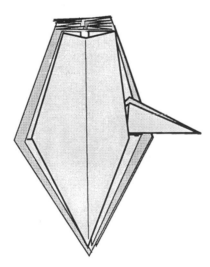

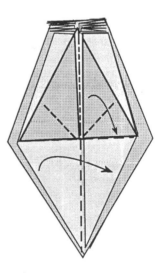

5. Repeat folding the petal on the remaining flaps.

4. Fold the petal by mountain folding the underside and folding it over to the side. Cover with the flap on the other side.

6. The Pentagon Frog Base Daffodil.

Chapter 4 BLINTZED BIRD BASE FLOWERS

The Blintzed Bird Base

The blintz operation consists of folding the four corners to the center of the paper. Folding a bird base or a frog base with the paper blintzed, results in the potential for eight points or petals. There are complications, such as the need to sink the center point, the unblintzing operation to transform the folded in corners into petals resembling the others already folded. Many complex animals with four legs, a head and tail entail the use of the blintzed bird base. With flowers there is the additional need to lock in the base of petals in order to keep the flower from opening up. I had developed these techniques many years ago. In my Origami Diary for June 11, 1966 I have a note that I was working on a six petal flower, which was accomplished by hiding two of the points. It also mentioned making the center of the eight petal flower a different color by bringing the underside of the petal to the top. Then I worked on the 16 petal chrysanthemum by folding each of the eight petals into two petals. Thus making a flower has meant for me using the blintzed bird or blintzed frog base.

The Eight Petal Flower

I have, perhaps cowardly, not given names to many of the flowers that I have folded. The eight petal flowers are daisy-like flowers. Two means of making the center white are provided. One involves turning the flower over and opening out the white side of the petal. Another is to reverse the color when starting to fold so that the center ridges are white. Then shorten the petals so that the ridges show through.

The Sixteen Petal Flowers

By blintz folding it was possible to increase the number of petals by four. By double blintzing--i.e. blintzing a second time, it is possible to increase the number of petals to 12. This is not a satisfactory gain in the number of petals since the amount folding necessary is increased a great deal. On the other hand, simply by folding petals in half it is possible to get sixteen petals. This method differs from a previous one I have used

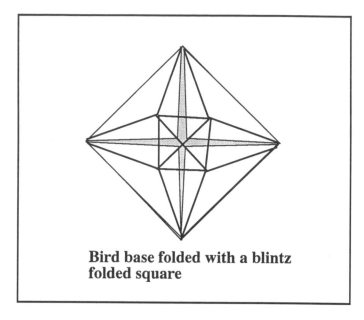

Bird base folded with a blintz folded square

until recently, since the extra petals were not fully formed. The bi-level sixteen petal flower is achieved by lifting the positions of the main petals. Its shape was modified to create what I have called a hydrangea-like flower. Of course, it is much simpler than a real hydrangea.

Blintzed Frog Base Flowers

Flowers with eight petals can also be folded from the frog base. The advantage of the frog base is that it provides a narrow tube underneath, which can also be turned upside-down and used as a cup in the center of the flower. Directions for these are given in the next chapter for the six petal version of the blintzed bird base.

The Eight Petal Flower Base

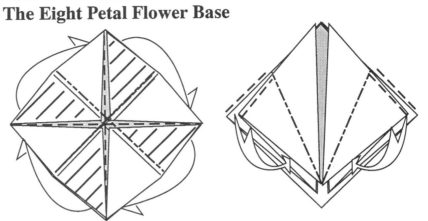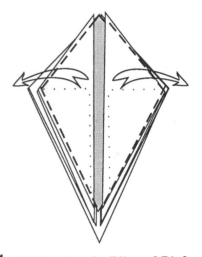

1. Blintz Fold. Start with a square whose corners have been folded in on the colored side. Flip over.

2. Fold the **square preliminary fold.** One way to do this is to first valley fold the lines to the corners and mountain fold the lines to the sides. Then accordion pleat around the edges into the center.

3. Inside reverse fold the four flaps to fold the bird base.

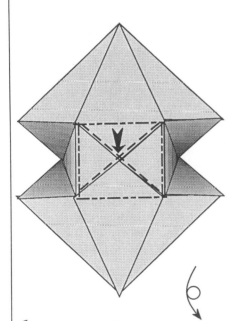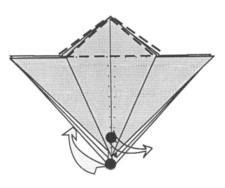

5. Stretching the Unblintzed Bird Base. Grasp the front and rear corners of the bird base and pull apart, flattening out the center square.

4. Unblintzing the Blintzed Bird Base. Fold out the four corners of the blintz fold.

6. Sinking the Center Point. Make mountain fold creases around the center square. Then prepare to push down its center. But first flip over to the underside.

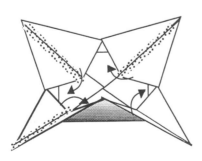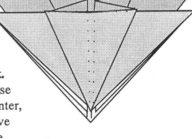

7. Four-way Lock. To make flower whose petals cling to the center, it is necessary to move bottom corners of the four flaps into their own slots as the center is being sunk. Hold one corner in position as you move the next one.

8. The Blintzed Bird Base unblintzed, center sunk and the flaps locked. This will be referred to as the **Eight Petal Flower Base.**

Eight Petal Flowers

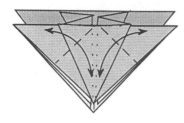

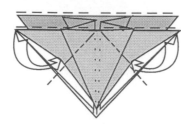

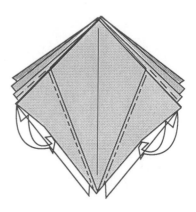

1. Start with the **Eight Petal Flower Base**. Fold the tops of each of the flaps along the center line. Then unfold.

2. Inside reverse fold each of the four flaps inserting the upper edge along the center line.

3. Inside Reverse Fold. Inside reverse fold each of the eight raw edges along the center line.

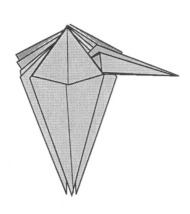

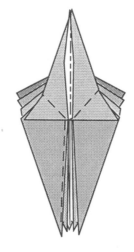

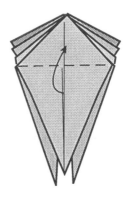

6. Complete the remainder of the petals and open out the petals.

5. Petal Bending. Inside reverse fold the raised flap to form a petal that extends horizontally. Cover with the adjoining flap.

4. Eight Petal Bird Base. Fold up the front flap as far as it will go.

7. Eight Petal Flower with Center Ridges. For a variation flip over.

8. Open out the colored covering on the petals to reveal the white paper.

9. White Eight Petal Flower.

16 Petal Chrysanthemum

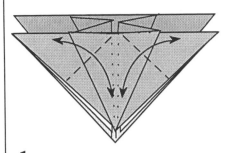

1. Start with the **Eight Petal Flower Base.** Make preliminary diagonal creases on both sides. Unfold.

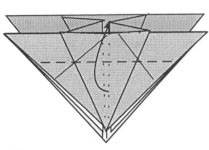

2. Fold up the front and back flaps across the two crosspoints.

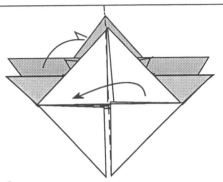

3. Bookfold (like turning pages of a book) front and back.

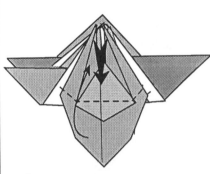

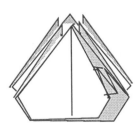

5. Book fold one flap into a vertical position and open out the sides.

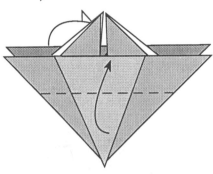

4. Fold up the front and back flaps.

6. Squash down on the center ridge and fold up the bottom corner.

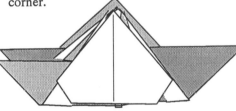

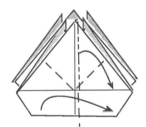

8. Make a crease across from corner to corner.

9. Fold a petal and cover it with an adjoining flap for a wide petal treatment.

7. Repeat Steps 5 and 6 on the remaining three flaps.

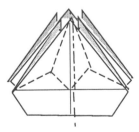

11. Complete the petals for the remaining seven flaps. Then open them out.

10. An alternative petal treatment. Fold the sides to cover the underside with colored paper. This produces a narrower petal.

12. The 16 Petal Chrysanthemum

White Center Flower

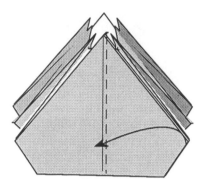

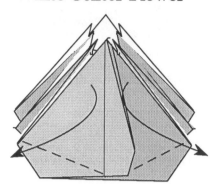

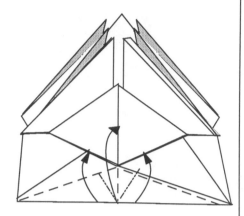

1. Start with the colors reversed in the 16 Petal Chrysanthemum and fold up through Step 8. Fold one flap into a vertical position.

2. Open out the flaps on both sides to work on the white side of the paper.

3. Fold in the lower edge with the center falling on the ridge.

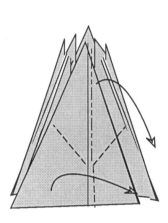

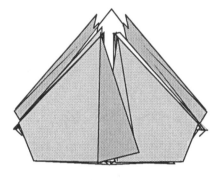

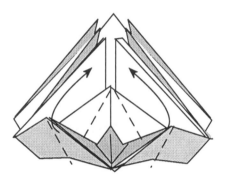

5. Repeat Steps 2 - 4 on the remaining flaps seven times.

4. Fold in the flaps back into its original positions.

6. Fold a petal out horizontally with the base determined by where the petal is caught inside.

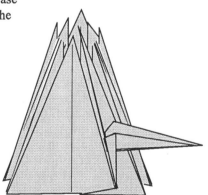

7. Repeat folding the petal on the remaining seven flaps.

8. White Center Flower.

Sixteen Bi-level Petal Flowers

By raising the level of eight of the petals, it is possible to make flatter petals on two levels.

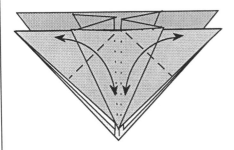

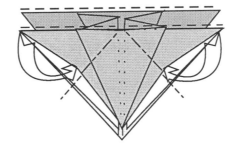

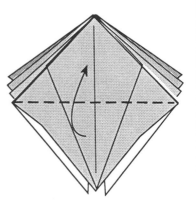

1. Start with the Eight Petal Flower Base. Fold and unfold each of the flaps with the top edge along the center line.

2. Inside reverse fold inserting the upper edge along the center line.

3. Fold up one of the flaps.

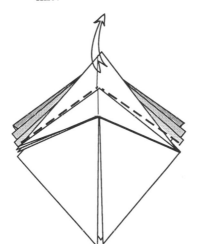

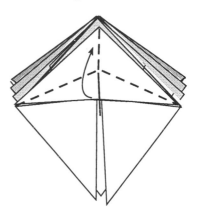

6. Starting from the raised position inside reverse fold the flap

5. Pull up on the corner of the flap to stretch it out.

4. Fold up the folded edge so that all angles are bisected. Squeeze the two sides together once to press in the creases.

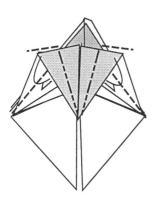

7. Complete folding of the petal by folding in the sides to the center line. Repeat Steps 3-7 for remaining seven flaps.

8. The 16 bi-level petal flower.

9. Hydrangea-like flower. Squeeze the ends of the lower level petals to flatten them. Then fold under the ends of all petals.

Chapter 5 SIX PETAL BLINTZED BIRD BASE FLOWERS

The Need for Six Petals

Some flowers, such as lilies and daffodils, come with six petals. Using four petals seem not enough and eight might be deemed too many by some. To get six petals from the eight provided by the blintzed bird or frog bases, I folded in or cut off two of the blintzed flaps. Folding can then proceed pretty much as for eight and sixteen petal flowers, except for one adjustment: the gaps left by the missing flaps need to be mended, calling for additional instructions.

Because of the complexity in the folding of the blintz bird and blintz frog bases, particularly for the six petal versions, it is probably preferable in many situations to work with the pentagons and hexagons. The petals are generally shorter than for the bird and frog bases, but still quite adequate for many flowers.

The Six Petal Flowers

The base for the six petal flower is the blintz fold with two opposing flaps cut off. The preliminary fold is carried out as usual and the center point is sunk with the petals locked in place. At this point a difficult sink of the corners where flaps have been cut off is necessary. The flower can then be completed either with the petals colored or the flower turned upside down and the white petals exposed.

The Six Petal Frog Base

The frog base can be folded in the usual fashion most of the way. Toward the end there is a need to lock in the connection where the flap has been removed. The base is shown with the sharp center point sunk in partially. This provides the necessary hold into which a stem is later inserted. It can also be used as the center cup of a flower like the daffodil.

The Six Petal Lily and Iris

The lily and iris can both be folded easily from the six petal frog base. The lily is folded with the petals bent over, while the iris has three of the petals pointed upward.

The Daffodil and Narcissus

The center cup of the daffodil is created by turning the six petal frog base upside down and the petals are folded in the usual manner. To make the white center for the narcissus the center hexagon is sunk and then countersunk.

The white petal version of the Six Petal Flower

The Narcissus with a white center.

Six Petal Bird Base

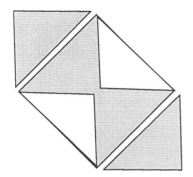

1. Half Blintz Fold. Start with a square whose corners have been folded in on the colored side, but with an opposing pair of blintz folds cut off.

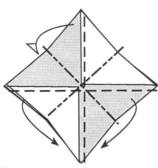

2. Fold the **square preliminary fold.** One way to do this is to first valley fold to the corners and mountain fold to the sides.

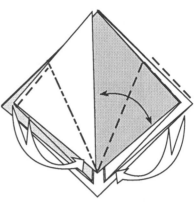

3. Inside reverse fold the two flaps with the blintz fold attached. Simply put in creases for the other two flaps.

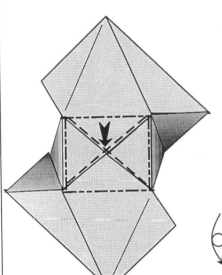

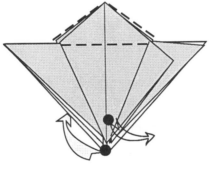

5. Stretching the Unblintzed Bird Base. Grasp the front and rear corners and pull apart, flattening out the center square.

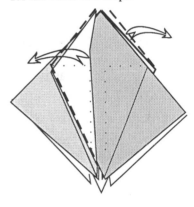

4. Unblintzing operation. unfold the two corners of the blintz folds by flipping the raw edges out to the sides.

6. Sinking the Center Point. Make mountain fold creases around the center square. Then push down its center. It is not necessary to perform the locking operation.

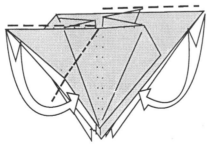

7. The Half Blintzed Bird Base unblintzed and the center sunk. Inside reverse fold the two unblintzed flaps.

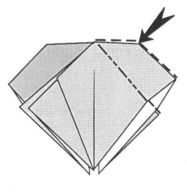

8 Make a preliminary diagonal crease. Then push in upper corner hard for a difficult sink and inside reverse fold. Repeat on remaining flap.

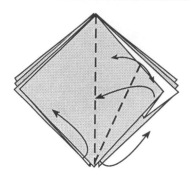

9 Fold the raw edges to the center line and unfold. Then open out the flaps on both sides

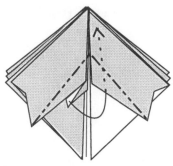

10. Inside reverse fold along the crease lines and then insert the excess fold all the way into the center. Repeat this locking operation on the remaining place where the blintz fold was cut off.

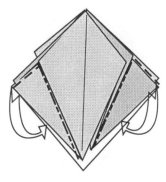

11. Inside reverse fold the remaining four flaps.

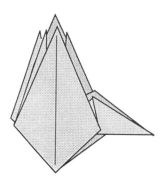

14 Complete the remaining petals.

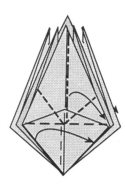

13 Fold the usual petal into a horizontal position and cover with the adjoining flap.

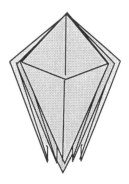

12 The Six Petal Bird Base. Turn upside down.

15. **The Six Petal Flower.**

14 **The White Petal Version.**

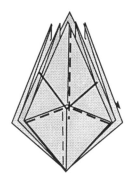

13. For a white petal valley fold along the length of the petal and topple to one side. Then open out the petals to show the white paper.

Six Petal Frog Base

One reason for going to six petals rather than to stick to eight is that some flowers, notably the lily, the iris and the daffodils, come with six petals. For these the frog base is more suitable than the bird base because it provides a trumpet like form.

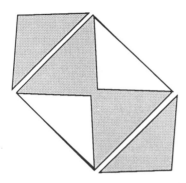

1. Half Blintz Fold. Start with a square whose corners have been folded in on the colored side, but with an opposing pair of blintz folds cut off.

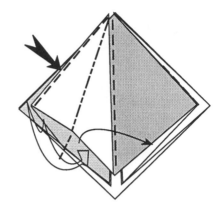

2. Fold the **square preliminary fold.** One way to do this is to first valley fold to the corners and mountain fold to the sides.

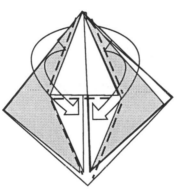

5. Pull out the blintz folded flap.

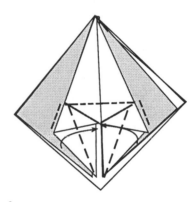

3. Squash fold the folded edge of the flap with the blintz fold attached.

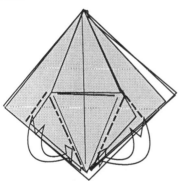

6. Inside reverse fold the pulled out flap.

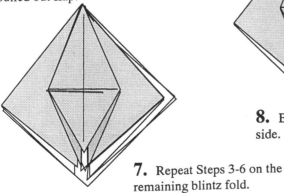

7. Repeat Steps 3-6 on the remaining blintz fold.

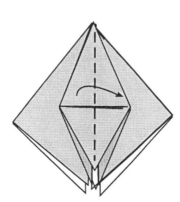

8. Book fold the flap to one side.

4. Fold in the lower edges to the center line and tuck under the center short flap.

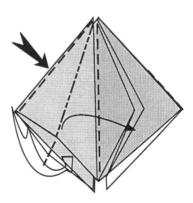

9. Squash fold the flap on the folded edge.

Six Petal Frog Base--2

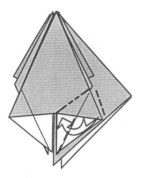

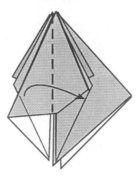

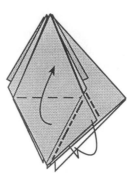

10. Start of operation to bind the two sides together. Inside reverse fold the raw edge on the right side all the way into the center line

11. Fold over the left side to be bound to the right side, bring the two sides to be bound together.

12. Fold up the lower half and allow the side to fold in.

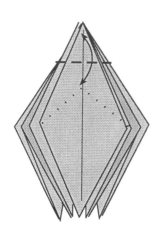

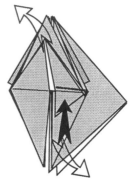

14. Repeat Steps 8-13 on the unfolded flap in the back.

13. To lock in the binding neatly pull apart the top and bottom flaps and push in the excess in between toward the center.

15. The Six Petal Frog Base. To sink the center point first make a crease by folding the center point to the top of the bird base hidden below. Then open out as flat as possible.

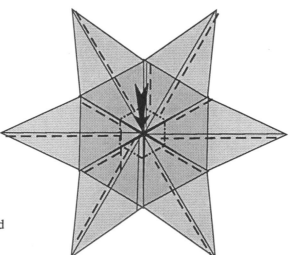

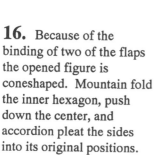

16. Because of the binding of two of the flaps the opened figure is coneshaped. Mountain fold the inner hexagon, push down the center, and accordion pleat the sides into its original positions.

17. The Six Petal Frog Base with a Sunken Center.

Six Petal Frog Base Lily

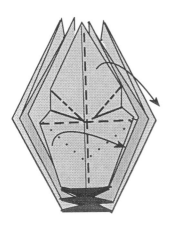

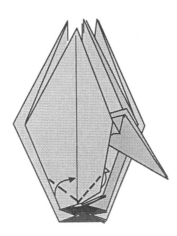

1. Start with the six petal frog base with the center sunk. Fold a petal with an accordion pleat at the base. Then cover with the adjoining flap.

2. Complete all of the petals and then fold the corner of the base to narrow the center hole. Open out the petals, allowing them to overlap and bend downward.

3. The Lily from the Six Petal Frog Base.

Six Petal Iris

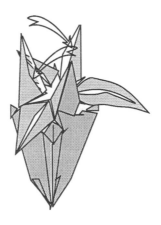

1. Start with the Lily. Lift up every other petal in its folded position.

2. For variation open out the white portion of the upright petals.

3. The Iris from the Six Petal Frog Base.

The Six Petal Daffodil

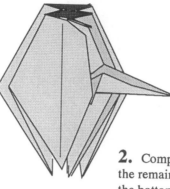

1. Start with the Six Petal Frog Base with a sunken center. Fold a petal as shown and cover with the adjoining flap.

2. Complete the folding of the remaining five petals. Fold the bottom sufficiently to narrow the center hole and to keep the petals together.

3. The Daffodil.

The Narcissus With A White Center

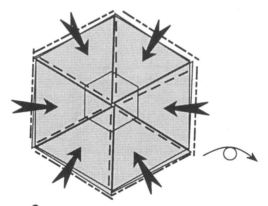

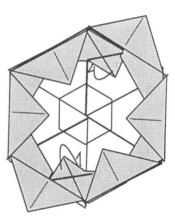

1. Start with Step 16 the Six Petal Frog Base opened out almost flat. Mountain fold under the outer petals.

2. Sink the larger hexagon. Flip over.

3. Locate the flaps holding two sides together and mountain fold under the excess triangle.

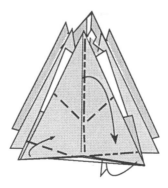

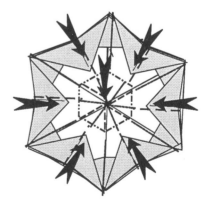

6. The Narcissus with a white center.

5. Check to see that two adjacent flaps share the paper at the base equally. Then form six petals and fold the bottom corner sufficiently to narrow the center hole and hold the petals together.

4. Accordion pleat the outside and countersink the inner hexagon.

Chapter 6 *THE SWIRL ROSE*

The Swirl Base

There seems to be a special attraction for the rose, and I have seen several attempts to fold it-- some of which were excellent. My work on the rose came, not as a deliberate attempt, but one that arose out of having worked with the base which I called the Swirl base. I have the following entry in my Origami Diary for September 6, 1970.

The box of folded contributions sent out by Thelma Mason included the Christmas ball by Fred Rohm and a two-toned six pointed star by Lewis Simon. One had started with an octagon and the other with a hexagon, but both used a flattened base and toppled over sides, which I have called the swirl base. It was a new base to me and I spent some time exploring it. One thing that occurred to me was the important characteristic of the swirl base was its long sides, which I tried to bring out. Fred made elaborate decorations on the top and bottom and hid the sides. Lewis Simon developed techniques in dealing with the swirl, some of which I used, but he flattened the figure and did not bring out the sides effectively. I started with a square, used a frog base, bent over the corners to obtain an octagon, and flattened out the figure into the swirl base. Basically, I used Simon's technique of folding around the edges, except that I left the edges more rounded, and then made a star in the center to make the swirl. Many people have commented on how lovely it looked, and also noticed that it was a different style than I've used previously. I've made a number of variations, but an important one was the impression of a rose, made by flattening the swirl so that the center star is low and lifting up the ridges to form rose-petals.

The Improved Rose

When I tried to make a rose from the swirl this time, I noticed that the result was not too impressive because of its flatness. I then bent the corners of the center star, and gave it a good twist, and this caused the rose to have more depth. By varying the degree of tightness of the twist of the center, the flower could be varied in size from a smallish bud to a larger flower. The touch that gives the rose its characteristic is the bending back of the petals.

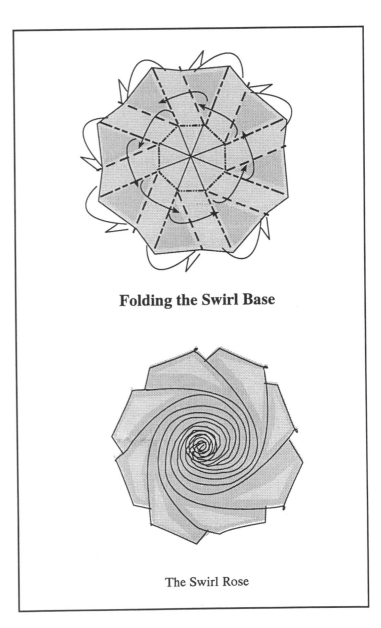

Folding the Swirl Base

The Swirl Rose

Rose from the Swirl

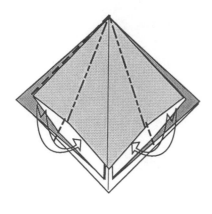

1. Start with the square preliminary fold. Inside reverse fold the folded edges as one would for the frog base.

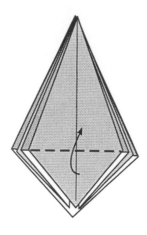

2. Fold up one triangular flap.

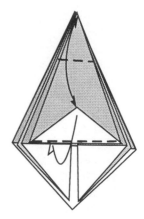

3. Fold down the top to the triangular flap and unfold. Then fold under all triangular flaps and fold out the octagon.

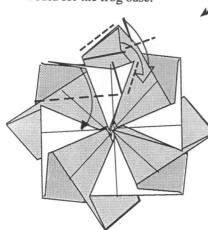

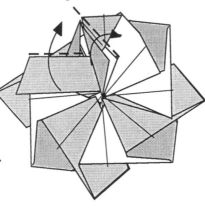

5. Flip over to the underside.

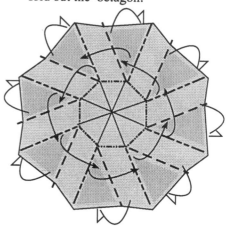

4. Mountain fold the edges of the inner octagon and accordion pleat each folded wedge parallel to the edge ahead. Tucking the triangular wedge under will force most of the outer edge under the inner octagon.

6. Fold down one edge to the crease below. At the same time squash fold the corner above.

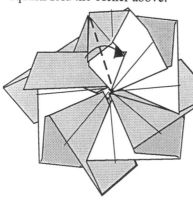

8. Flip over the triangular piece just folded and at the same time lift up the edge which was folded down to its original position.

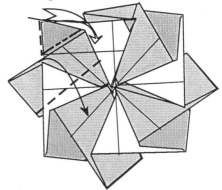

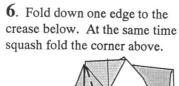

7. Fold over the naffow triangular piece.

9. Repeat Steps 6-8 on the remaining edges, working counter-clockwise.

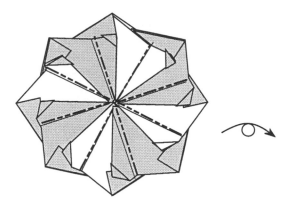

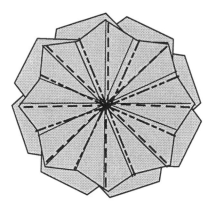

10. Mountain fold the creases and then turn the figure over.

11. Accordion pleat the octagon with valley folds to the corners and mountain folds to the sides.

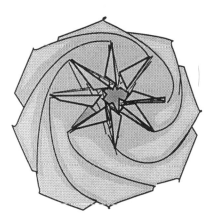

13. Hold the bottom of the swirl and give the center core a strong twist to provide the rose with some depth. Then shape the petals by folding back their outer edges.

12. The Swirl. To make the rose first fold in the corners of the inner octagon, working counter-clockwise.

14. Rose from the Swirl.

Chapter 7 FREE FORM ORIGAMI

Offset Bird Base

Making lengths of petals unequal helps to provide desirable variations. One method of doing this was to move the center of the square paper toward one corner, providing one longer and one shorter than normal petals. (See Modern Origami by James M. Sakoda, Simon and Schuster, 1969). It has been used to create a bird with a longer neck, a tallish mask, a long dachshund. Its best application was in the blintz bird base, which allowed for six staggered legs for an insect.

The difficulty with the offset bird base on some occasion is that it is not "perfect", using Jacques Justin's term. Two of the flaps are caught in the center and are not able to move up and down freely. Hence, it is not suitable for forming flowers.

The Perfect Bird Base

Jacques Justin of France in a mathematical paper defined a perfect bird base as one which allows all four flaps to move freely up and down. The paper is titled Mathematical Remarks About Origami Bases (1982). To accomplish this it is necessary to cut a non-square form which maintains the following relationship among the four sides, a, b, c, and d.

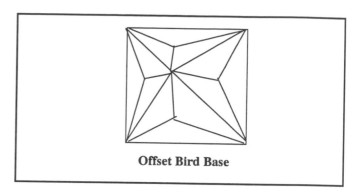

Offset Bird Base

Types of Free form

Any kite or diamond shape will meet the free-form restriction. It is bilaterally symmetric and provides one short and one long petal. The trapezoid is bilaterally symmetric also, but provides two long and two short points side by side, as one would see in a frog base. In the general case, it is possible to make all four sides or points of unequal lengths, but these can lean either toward the kite or trapezoid forms. For flowers, either can be used.

Cutting the Free Form Paper

For the general case in which all four sides are of different lengths there is a single cut method of construction, which I learned from Professor Husimi of Japan (coauthor of *Origami no Kikagaku* or **The Geometry of Origami**.). It can be seen from the illustration that the desired measurements are achieved. Detailed instructions are provided for folding the paper and making the cut

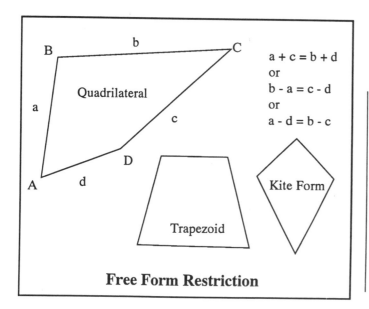

$$a + c = b + d$$
or
$$b - a = c - d$$
or
$$a - d = b - c$$

Free Form Restriction

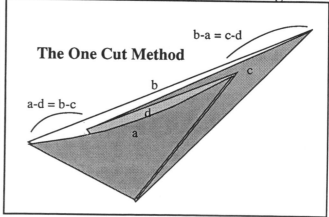

The One Cut Method

for the free form of one's choice.

Locating the Free Form Center

After the free form paper, with unequal sides, is cut, there is still the task of finding the center which allows for the folding of the perfect bird base. In his remarkable paper Jacques Justin has shown that the desired center, which he called Point of Loiseau, is the crosspoint of two hyperbolas. A suitable definition of a hyperbola for our purpose is that for any point on the curve, the difference in the distances to the two foci is a constant. If A and C are the foci and B and D are points on the hyperbola, then BC - BA = DC - DA. It is convenient that the quadrilateral was constructed so that this condition would hold. We seek a Point O near the center such that OC -OA = BC - BA or CD - AD. Similarly the second hyperbola has B and D as foci and extend from A to C and AB - AD = OB - OD = CB - CD.

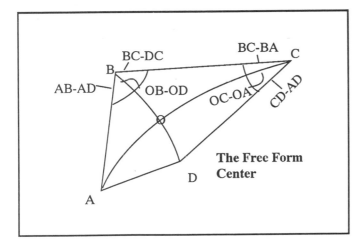

The Free Form Center

Folding with Free Form Paper

Folding the preliminary fold, the bird base, the frog base as well as the windmill base can proceed pretty much as with a square piece of paper. The main difference is that precreasing cannot be done simultaneously for two corners, but each one has to be done separately. If done together there needs to be an adjustment later for one of them.

Jacques Justin did not cover the blintz bird situation, but I have found that the blintz bird and frog bases can be folded without much difficulty. Folding in the four corners produces a quadrilateral which appears to meet the free form restriction rather closely. It is possible to recalculate a new center of this quadrilateral, but I have found this generally not to be necessary.

Some Sample Results

The degree of departure from equal petal lengths can be varied. Small variations can pass almost unnoticed, and may appear quite natural. More extreme variations may be used on occasion as an attention getting mechanism. Below are shown two examples of free form flowers. Both are based on the blintzed bird base. Incidentally, these procedures cannot be applied to the pentagon or the hexagon.

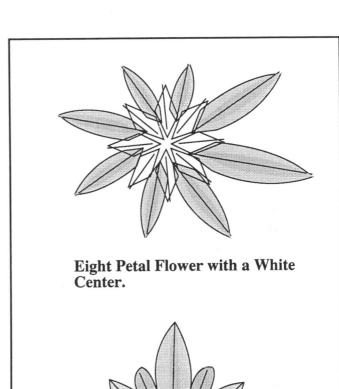

Eight Petal Flower with a White Center.

16 Petal Chrysanthemum

Free Form Choices

One can choose, not only the degree of differences among the sides, but also the shapes they take---kite form, trapezoid or general free form in which all four sides vary in length. Start by folding a diagonal and a horizontal center line. The center of the paper represents a square or a diamond. Departing from it will produce increasingly asymmetrical forms.

Kite Form

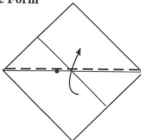

K1. Locate a spot on the diagonal line. A moderate deviation is 1/8 of the distance from the center to the corner. Fold along the diagonal line.

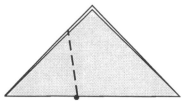

K2. Fold from the spot to the raw edge so that the edge points to the far corner.

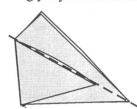

K3. Make a straight cut along the upper edge so that the cut goes through all four levels. Open out.

K4. The Kite Form

Trapezoid Form

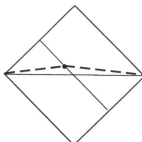

T1. Locate a spot on the horizontal center line. Fold from the left corner to the spot, and then from the spot to the right corner.

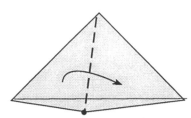

T2. Fold from the spot to the upper corner of the top layer.

T3. Two of the raw edges should be parallel and the differences between the corners at both ends should be the same. Make a straight cut through four layers and open out.

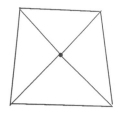

T4. The Trapezoid Form.

General Form (a and b)

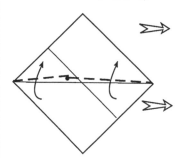

G1. Choose a point between the two lines. Then fold from the left corner to the spot and then from the spot to the right corner.

a   b

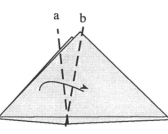

G2a. Fold from the spot to the upper edge so that when folded it points to the right corner.

G2b. Fold from the spot to the upper corner as one would for a trapezoid.

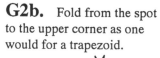

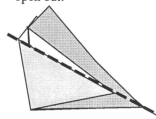

G3a. Cut along the upper edge through all four layers. Then open out.

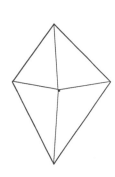

G4 a. The general free form kite form.

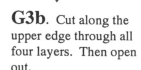

G3b. Cut along the upper edge through all four layers. Then open out.

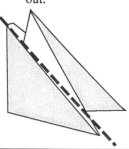

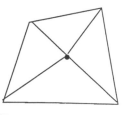

G4b. The general free form trapezoid.

Free Form Preliminary Fold

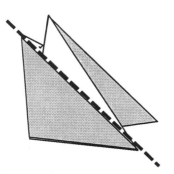

1. Start with a square given a free form cut. Here we use the trapezoid form as an example.

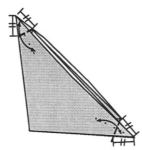

2. At each corner imagine an angle bisector and fold down the corner on that line beginning where the shorter corner ends. Unfold them both. This transfers the differences from the edge to the center line.

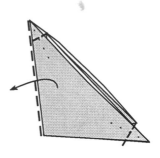

3. Open out into a non-flat triangle.

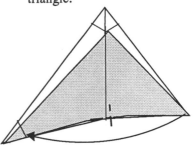

4. Fold over the short corner at the base to the ends where the two creases meet and make a short crease to mark the position of the new center as measured from one corner.

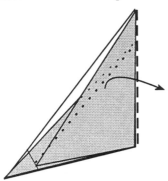

6. Open out into a non-flat triangle.

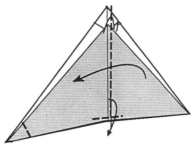

5 Place the top corner on the ends of the two creases and make a new crease at the base. The cross point marks the position of the new center. Fold over from the new center to the top.

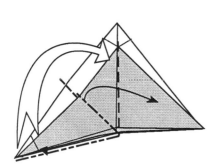

7. Instead of making a preliminary crease go directly for a squash fold. Open out the flap and fold the lower corner to the new center line. Then press down flat.

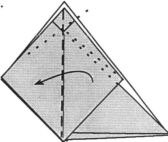

8. Fold over a flap to avoid the need to turn the paper over.

11. **The Free Form Preliminary Fold.** If folded correctly the side corners will line up along a horizontal straight line which is perpendicular to the vertical line to the four corners.

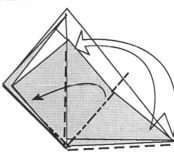

9. Squash fold the remaining flap along the new center line.

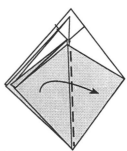

10. Fold back one flap to leave two on each side.

Free Form Bird and Frog Bases

With only a little exception after the preliminary fold is completed for the free form paper, the bird base, frog base and others can be folded in the usual manner. The main difference is that the petals are of different lengths.

Free Form Bird Base

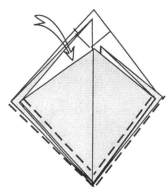

1. Start with the free form preliminary base. Because flaps are of unequal lengths, bypass the preliminary crease and open out the figure.

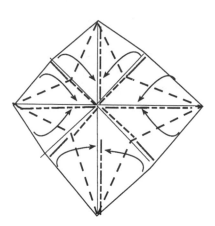

2. Fold the side to the two closest center lines. When all are completed fold together into a bird base. Notice that each petal is covered on the underside completely and that the flaps can move freely.

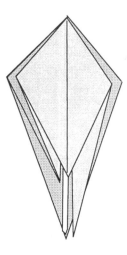

3. The Free Form Bird Base. If properly folded the side corners will line up horizontally in a straight line.

Free Form Frog Base

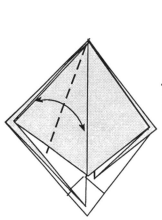

1. Start with the free form preliminary form. Make a preliminary crease by folding the folded edge to the center line. Unfold.

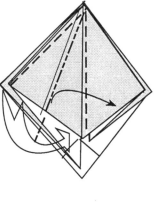

2. Squash fold the folded edge to the center line.

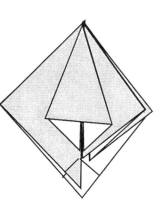

3. Repeat on the remaining three flaps.

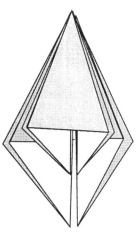

4. The Free Form Frog Base, still incomplete.

The Free Form Blintzed Preliminary Fold

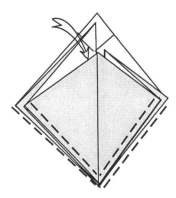

1. Start with the free form preliminary fold. Open out completely.

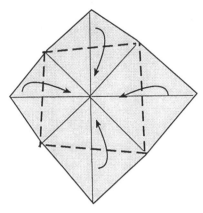

2. Use the ends of the crease lines to fold in the corners (blintz fold). Some corners do not reach the center, while others go beyond it.

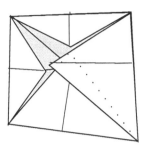

3. Flip over to the other side.

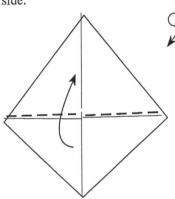

4. Follow the crease lines and fold up the bottom corner.

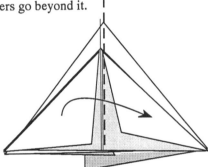

5. Fold over the left corner.

6. The four diagonal edges should line up as though given a free form cut. At this point it is possible to recalculate a new free form center, but differences are generally small and the correction usually unnecessary. Proceed with the squash fold.

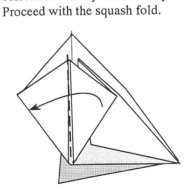

7. Flip back one flap.

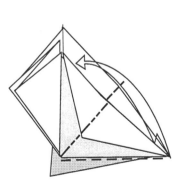

8. Repeat the squash fold and flip back on the other side.

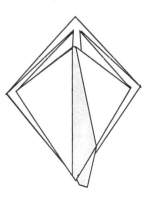

9. The Free Form Blintzed Preliminary Fold. From here one can preceed as usual with the blintz bird or blintz frog base routines. The extra long flaps will be straightened out when they are unblintzed. Notice that what started out as a trapezoid form becomes a kite form.

Chapter 8   SIMPLE BIRD BASE FLOWERS

Simple Bird Base Flowers

In the September-October issue of FOLD for 1992 I reported on the discovery of the rose and tulip, both based on the bird base and relatively simple to fold but still attractive. The occasion was a comment by Rachel Katz, one of the participants in the origami newsletter exchanged six times a year among two dozen people and who had read the first desktop published edition of the Origami Flower Arrangement. She said that the section titled Beginning Lessons on Paper Folding was misleading in that it was not all that easy. She must have had trouble with the modification of the traditional frog base lily, the traditional flower available for beginners. The modification involved flipping out four white little squares in the center of the lily involving some new unfamiliar moves (See Pages 23-24).

The idea of using the twist for the rose was already familiar to me, since I had worked on the more complex swirl rose. It did not take me long to develop the bird base version, which I followed with the tulip, which came to me easily. The initial move of folding up the flaps also provided a convenient hole for insertion of a stem, making it unnecessary to sink the center point to provide for a hole, as one would for the traditional frog base lily. The tulip as well as the lily belong to the bulb family of flowers which call for long leaves, providing a contrast with other flowers requiring smaller and more conventional leaves. Because of their simplicity both flowers can be folded from five inch square paper, and four of them can be cut from a sheet of 10 inch square paper. For these reasons the two flowers are the easiest with which to begin learning the flower arrangement process.

Pentagon Versions

Both the rose and the tulip can be folded without much modification from a pentagon instead of a square. For the rose it is only necessary to fold down the lifted petals 1/3 rather than 1/2 of the distant to the bottom. Otherwise, the folding can follow the instructions given for the bird base versions. Both are more attractive and natu-ral-looking than the simpler bird base version. I usually fold pentagon based flowers with a six inch square or larger because of the loss from the cutting operation. This is also true of folding from a blintzed bird base, which results in a smaller flower because of the blintzing operation. By using the pentagon cut from a square sheet it is possible to fold an acceptable bird base rose and tulip, even though they are somewhat smaller in size.

The Improved Easy Pentagon

I have been folding the pentagon using a method I found in Koji and Mitsue Husimi's **Origami no Kikagaku (The Geometry of Origami)**, which I used in Chapter 5. The method is relatively simple to use. Recently came across Haga's Theorem in Kunihiko Kasahara's **Origami Omnibus** (1988) and I became interested in using it as an easy method of folding the maximum pentagon. With only two folds a 3x4x5 right triangle is formed at one corner for which the claim is made that the hypotenuse of is 5/8 the length of the side of the square and is the side of a maximum pentagon fit into a square. By moving this side to one corner across the diagonal line it supposedly is possible to fold a pentagon of maximum size. I asked Roberto Morassi whether he had used Haga's theorem and he said that he had not and said that Haga's approach only provided a close approximation, with an error of .001179 for the length of the side. From a practical point of view of a folder this amount of error is of little consequence, since the folding procedure itself is apt to produce small amounts of errors. However, it requires moving the 5/8th line to a diagonal position on the sheet, not an easy folding task.

In Issue 188 for February, 1998 of the British Origami Ian Harrison in his Workshop section presented a variety of methods of folding the pentagonal angle. Using a pair of 3 x 4 x 5 right triangles (same one used by Haga), he calculated that the combined smaller angle of 53.13, when doubled added up to 106.26, an approximation to 108 degrees. Actual trials using the two pentagonal sides as a basis for folding the pentagon proved that the method is simple, leaves only a few creases not needed for the folding the bird base, but was not accurate enough for the consistent creation of a decent pentagon. I have calculated the error in using 5/8 or .6250 as the length of the side of a pentagon as .6250 - .6180 = .0070 of the widest point, which in this case is 1.0. For a 6.25 inch square the correction is 7/10th of 1/16th of an inch. This means that the pentagon becomes a little short of the maximum possible. The method generally works even when the correction is approximate.

The use of the 3 x 4 x 5 right triangle is attractive for its simplicity as well as the fact that the 3x4x5 right triangle has the simple relatonship among the squares of its sides:

$$3^2 + 4^2 = 5^2 \text{ or } 9 + 16 = 25.$$

Haga's approach can be used to find other odd divisions.

Using the pentagon it is possible to fold the rose and the tulip from a five inch square. The flowers are a little smaller than working with the four petal bird base, but the appearance of the flowers is improved and four 5 inch squares can be cut from a ten inch square (See Figs.1 and 2)

Size of Paper

I generally use six inch square paper when starting with a pentagon or for flowers requiring blintz folding, as one would with flowers with six or eight petals. However, only one six inch square can be cut from a ten inch paper. For six petal flowers in which two of the blintz folds are cut off (see Chapter 5) it is possible to cut 10 inch squares in half and cut off the corners, as shown in Fig. 3 and fold two hexagon flowers.

Fig. 1. Pentagon v.s. Square Rose

Fig. 2. Square v.s. Pentagon Tulip

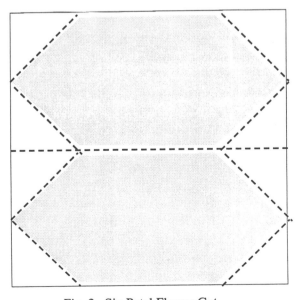

Fig. 3. Six Petal Flower Cut

Bird Base Rose

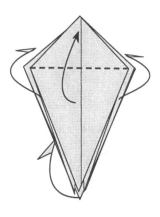

1. Start with the bird base. Fold up the front and back. Book-fold the front and then the back flaps and fold up the side flaps.

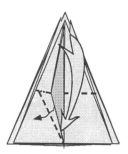

2. Fold the front flap in half first and then open out the left side and fold down the top . (When using a pentagon fold down only the top third.)

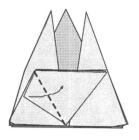

3. Fold in the opened side flap to lock the top flap in place. Repeat Steps 2 and 3 on the remaining sides.

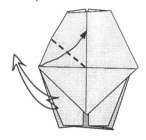

5. Pull out the flap on the left side and fold the left corner to the vertical center line. Working counter clockwise do the same for each of the other flaps in turn.

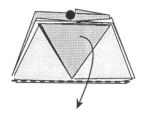

4. Hold the bottom flap and fold forward the rest.

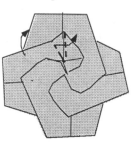

6. Increase the overlap with a second bend at the base. This step can be left out if a flatter rose is desired or the move is too troublesome.

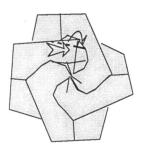

7. Fold under about 1/3 of the edge to make it rounder. Push down against the bend to make the petal curved. Repeat Steps 6 and 7 on the other 3 petals.

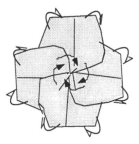

8. The Final Twist. First insert any stem into the hole on the underside before it is closed tight. Hold the bottom of the rose in the palm of the left hand and place fingers of the right hand between the center peak and twist three or four times. Then bend under the eight corners around the edges.

Bird Base Tulip

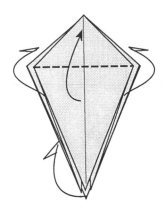

1. Start with the bird base. Fold up the front and back. Book-fold the front together and then the back flaps and fold up the side flaps.

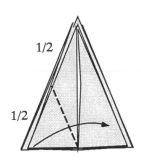

1/2

1/2

2. Fold the corner of the lefthand flap about 1/2 up the side.

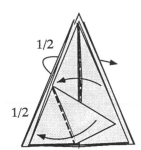

1/2

1/2

1/2

3. Unfold the corner and bookfold the lefthand flap in front to the left and the one in the back to the right. Repeat Steps 2 and 3 until all of the four flaps have preliminary diagonal creases.

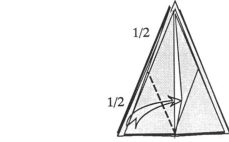

1/2

1/2

4. Insert the left corner flap into the pocket on the right.

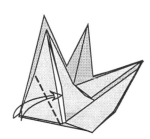

6. Inscrt the left corner. Continue pulling out the next flap and inserting the corner. Make the creases sharp to prevent corners from pulling out.

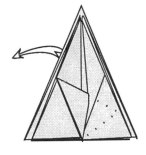

5. Pull out the next flap on the left.

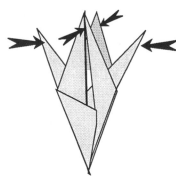

7. The Bird Base Tulip. Bend the end of the petals inward for a tulip-like effect.

8. The Bird Base Tulip

Improved Easy Pentagon

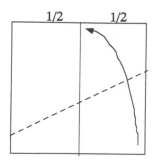

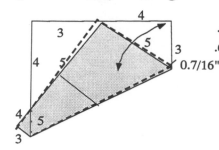

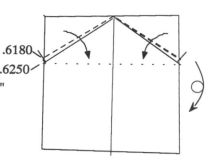

1. Start with a square paper uncolored side up, creased vertically in half. Fold the lower righthand corner to the top of the center line.

2. This shows Kazuo Haga's three 3x4x5 right triangles. Calculate the error in using Haga's 3x4x5 triangle by taking .6250 - .6180 = .0070 and multiplying by the size of the paper (6.25 inches) and multiply by 16 to get the error in 16th of an inch. This turns out to be 0.7. Locate the end of the shortened line and pull the corner beyond the top of the paper. Also only crease the top half inch or so of the diagonal line to avoid unnecesary creases.

3. Ian Harrison's double 3x4x5 right triangles can be used as two sides of a pentagon. The angle between the two sides is equal to 106.26 degrees and is an approximation of 108 degrees, the true value. Fold in the two top corners using the shortened lines on both sides. This should increase the angle between the two lines to close to 108°, the true value. Then flip the paper upside down.

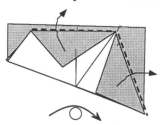

6. Fold over the two corner flaps. Then flip the paper over horizontally to allow showing the horizontal cut lines on both sides after the next folding is completed.

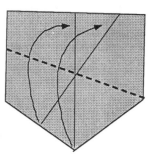

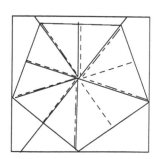

7. a. Fold the right lower corner to the nearest center line. b. Then fold over the left edge to meet the folded right edge. Check to see that the horizontal lines in front and back coincide.

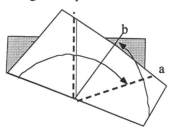

5. Fold the lower half starting at the end of the lower right corner through the central crosspoint, with the lower corner ending on the diagonal line and the diagonal line on the center line. The edge is parallel to the upper edge. If the lower corner does not meet the diagonal line, it probably means that the initial correction was insufficient.

4. Fold the left side lower edge in half and unfold making a diagonal crease.

10. To fold the bird base or frog base mountain fold the lines from the center to the corners and valley fold the lines to the sides. Then flip the paper over to the colored side.

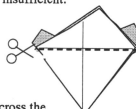

8. Fold or cut across the horizontal lines in front and back.

9. The **Improved Easy Pentagon** based on the work of Kazuo Haga and Ian Harrison.

Chapter 9

FOLDING VASES

Functions of the Vase

The folded vases described here serve more than the function of holding stems of flowers. In Japanese flower arrangement stems of flowers need to be shaped and positioned appropriately. Not only are they selected and cut to the right length, but are also forced to maintain a rigid position in relationship to one another. To hold the bottom of the stems in position a metal base with many sharp needles pointing upward called *kenzan* or frog is often placed at the bottom of the vase. If necessary at the top of the vase one or more twigs are placed across the top to help hold the stems in place. Our folded vases come with these capabilities already in place. On top a flexible center hole and slits to the corners can hold several stems in place. In the bottom grooves around the edges the stems can be inserted without bending and held in place securely with the aid of poster putty.

Vase Improvement

One of the difficulties of the first vases made of poster board was that they were too unstable, particularly when flowers and stems were extended out horizontally. I tried to overcome this by making the vase wide and squat, using 6 x 13 inch poster boards. This helped, but did not really solve the problem completely. I tried adding a wooden block on the bottom of the vase, but this would not have been acceptable to learners who did not have access to a table saw. Another difficulty was that its being 3.5 inches in height and 2.5 inches in width made it more appropriate for a low, horizontal arrangement than for a tall upright one. Another shortcoming was that the vase was chosen to be black since it originally suited the gold color of the wheat stalk arrangement, with which I began the flower arrangement.

Foil Covering for the Vase

To improve the appearance of the vase and to make it cleanable the poster board for vases is now covered with foil paper. The preferred color of the foil paper is silver with a small mosaic pattern of embossing. To attach the foil paper to the poster board any good paper glue probably will work, but

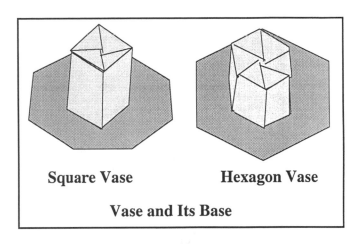

Square Vase **Hexagon Vase**

Vase and Its Base

my present preference is for Avery-Dennison's Permanent Glue Stick (large size), which goes on easily and holds well. For the vase it is only necessary to put the glue around the edges.

Size of the Poster Board

Previously the poster board was cut to 12 or 13 inch lengths, but with the need to use foil paper I have cut back the standard length to 10 inches, which would allow the use of foil paper already cut to 10 inch sizes. The standard width is now set to 5 inches, which would allow the 10 inch paper to be cut into two 5 x 10 inch pieces. As a result the square vase is now 2 inch wide and 3.5 inch tall. A taller vase could easily be made by making the foil paper and poster board 6 inches or more wide. The groove at the bottom is set at 5/8 inch, which is a minimum value to make the vase as tall as possible. Its width can be increased to make the vase wider and shorter. As it turns out after folding some arrangements, the 5 x 10 inch limitation appears to work out well for the average small arrangement.

The Hexagon Vase

To vary the shape of the vase, which also made it wider, a hexagon shape has been added to the square one. The general method of folding has not changed, but a new set of measurements are required. The hexagon vase measures 3 inches tall and 3 inches at its widest point, and has a squatter appearance than the square one. It is also more suitable for horizontal rather than upright arrangements.

Pentagon Vase

A pentagon vase is possible, following the directions for the other vases. For those who may be in need of a five-sided vase some hints are given here. First, fold six panels, by dividing the poster board into thirds and then into sixths. To find the width of the six panels fold a pentagon and cut off one of the wedges to the center of the pentagon. Then position this down the center of the first and last panels and mark the position where the wedge just fits the panels.

The Base for the Vase

In order to take care of the instability problem a base has been added to the bottom of the vase. It is wide enough to take care of the instability problem in general, regardless of the size or shape of the vase itself. For larger arrangements the vase and possibly the base should be made larger to hold the vase with the base and the arranged flowers. The base is made of poster board covered with foil paper and its color should be chosen not to clash with the flower arrangement. In gluing the poster board it is necessary to cover the entire area, since the inside and outside areas need to be cut. For the square base the outside is trimmed to an octagon, while for the hexagon vase a hexagon shape is used.

The inside is cut from corner to opposite corner to open a hole and also cut triangular flaps which are pushed upward inside the vase to hold it in place. The cutting is most easily done with a razor blade knife, with the poster board placed on a cutting board. To attach the triangular flaps to the vase poster putty is placed on the triangular pieces and pressed against the inside of the vase. The poster putty can also be put on the inside of the bottom ridge.

In origami there is a general distaste for gluing, but there are occasions when practical or artistic demands require them. They are less objectionable when their effects are not visible, as in this case. Poster putty, furthermore, involves temporary gluing, which is a useful device in modular origami in situations in which units put together are likely to be in danger of coming apart unexpectedly. There is also a folded device in place to hold pieces together which can usually be counted on to work.

On the other hand, the use of more permanent glue is not recommended because it prevents making changes.

Folding the Vase

I was surprised with the relative ease with which poster boards could be folded. However, it is not practical to fold poster boards just to get measurements. For this reason one should prepare a ruler or template with a strip of paper the same length or dimension as the poster board. The division into five or seven panels or the forming of a pentagon or hexagon can be done on the ruler or template. The measurements can then be transferred to the poster board. For the actual folding of the poster board, a straightedge should be used and the fold lines first scored with a wooden scoring tool or with one's thumbnail if it is strong enough. Press down on a ball point pen to score and draw a line simultaneously. The actual folding can be done with the straightedge in position, or if not, one can place fingernails of the forefingers on the line and fold over one side of the line with the two thumbs.

Shape of the Bottom Grooves

The grooves at the bottom of the vase plays an important role of keeping the stem bottom anchored. Previously there was a bend in the bottom fold which made the groove straight and tight. This made insertion of the stem difficult and served to bend and weaken it. Consequently. the horizontal bend has been replaced by a diagonal bend from one corner to the center. This provided a convenient opening for the stem. To insure that the stem stays in place poster putty is placed at the end of the stem, preferably inside a groove to facilitate the insertion or removal of the stem.

Other Uses for the Vase

The vase can be used for arranging dried flowers. In some cases it may be preferable to turn the open end up. In this form it is possible to use as a pencil holder, although a taller vase is desirable. Other origami creations, such as *Kusudama* (colorful balls), are often in need of a base for display purposes, and the vase might be useful. The vase can hold a stiff stem, which can serve as a pole from which to display some things.

The Square Vase Ruler

The basic square vase is made from a poster board measuring 5 by 10 inches, but can be made taller by increasing the width or wider by increasing the length. Whatever the length it needs to be folded into fifths. Since the poster board cannot be easily folded just to make measurements, it is desirable to fold a paper of the same dimension to measure out the one fifth positions as well as other measurements.

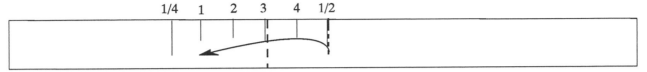

1. Start with paper the length of the poster board from which the vase is made. Fold in half to find the 1/2 mark and in half again to find the 1/4 mark. Divide the distance between the two by eye into fifths, numbered 1-4. Then check this by folding over the 1/2 mark at the third mark and see if it fall on the No. 1 mark.

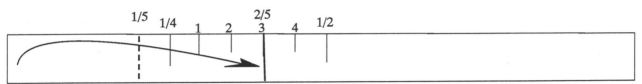

2. To find the locations of the first two 1/5th sections assume that each of the 1/4 segments are divided in fifths, giving 20 small units for the entire ruler. If we divide the 20 units by 5, we need one unit less in the first segment and 2 less in the second. The end of the second segment is at the No. 3 mark. Hence fold the left end on the No. 3 mark to establish the end of the first 1/5th segment.

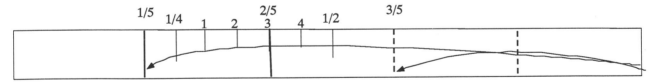

3. Fold the right edge to the 1/5th mark to locate the 3/5th mark. Then fold the edge to the 3/5th mark for the 4/5th mark.

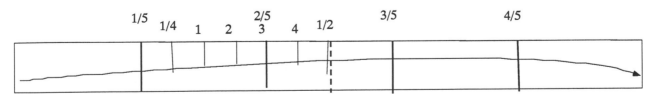

4. As a check fold at the 1/2 mark to see if the marks on the two sides coincide.

Square Vase

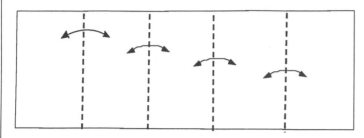

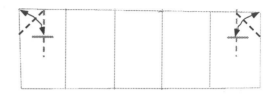

1. Take the poster board covered with foil paper and use the the Square Vase Ruler to mark off the five panels with valley folds. It is helpful to use a straight edge (ruler or another poster board) to make a crease with a creasing tool or one's thumb nail before folding.

2. To find the width of the top edge to be folded take the ruler and find the midpoint of the first and last segments. Then fold down the corner to the midpoint line and mark where the corner ends.

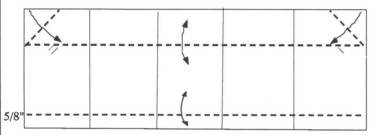

5/8"

Top View   **Bottom View**

3. a. Make a valley fold crease across the top from the mark on the left to the one on the right. b. At the bottom meaure out a minimum of 5/8th inch and make a valley fold crease across. This creates the grooves to hold the end of the stems.

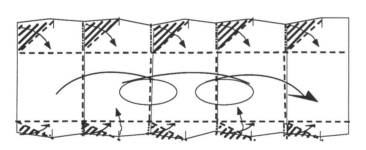

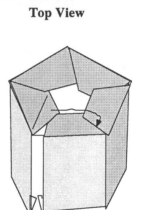

5. The Square Vase

4. Precreasing. a. Mark off the center of each of the panels at the top and bottom. Then put in valley fold creases along the diagonals, vertical mountain fold creases along the top and bottom. Use a straightedge and score the line before attempting to bend it. b. Starting at the left, fold in the top perpendicular to the side and tightly fold over each triangular shaded area in turn. Do the same for the bottom, except that the bottom ends are folded flat while the top ends are perpendicular to the sides.

5. Locking the Ends. a. Check to see that the valley and mountain folds have not reversed in the process of rolling up the vase. The end panels are overlapped, with the left side fitting on the outside of the right side. b. Hook the loose flap on top into the groove beneath. c. Push in the bottom folded edge against the inside of the vase to form the grooves to hold the stems. d. To make the top flat push up the pleats on top from the bottom, using a ruler.

The Hexagon Vase Ruler

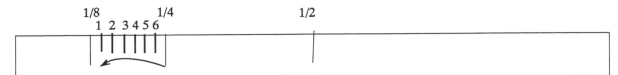

1. Start with a strip of paper the length of the poster board from which the vase is made. Fold in half to find the 1/2 point, in half again to find the 1/4 point, and in half a third time to find the 1/8th point. The second segment is assumed to represent the extra segment, which is divided into sevenths by eye and labeled 1 - 6. Fold the second 1/8th segment into two made up a of four units on one side and three on the other. As a check fold the 1/4 mark at the 4th mark and see if the mark falls on Mark No. 1. If it does not reestimate the division into 7 units and redo the estimation. One segment of the second eighth section is allotted to the first 1/7th section.

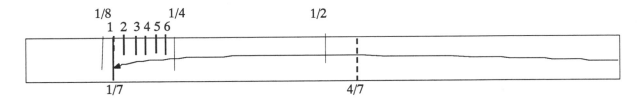

2. We need to identify the division line of the remaining six segments. Divide the remaining segments into half to determine the location of the 4/7th point.

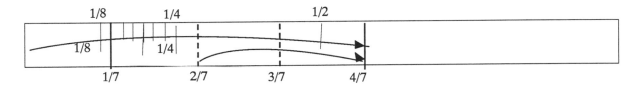

3. Then fold the left side of the 4/7th line to find the 2/7th line and fold the 2/7th line to the 4/7th line to find the 3/7th line.

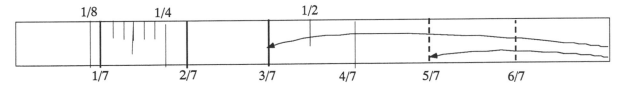

4. Then fold the right side to the 3/7th line. Then fold the end to the 5/7th line to find the 6/7th line.

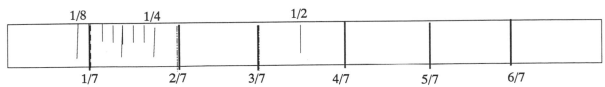

5. The completed ruler divided into sevenths. Fold in half to check if both sides are equally spaced.

Hexagon Vase

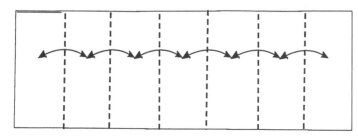

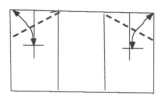

1. Take the poster board and using the Hexagon Vase Ruler mark off the seven panels and valley fold. It is helpful to use a straight edge (ruler or another poster board) to make a crease with one's thumb nail or a creasing tool before folding.

2 . To find the width of the top edge to be folded take a piece of paper and find the midpoint of the first and last segments. Then fold down the corner to the midpoint line and mark where the corner ends.

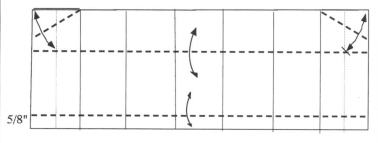

5/8"

3. a. Make a valley fold crease across the top from the mark on the left to the one on the right. b. At the bottom meaure out 5/8th inch and make a valley fold crease across. The smaller bend will increase the height of the vase just a little. This creates the grooves to hold the end of the stems.

Top View

Bottom View

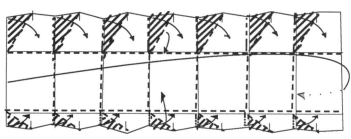

6. Hexagon Vase

4. Precreasing. a. Mark off the center of each of the panels at the top and bottom. Then put in valley fold creases along the diagonal lines and vertical mountain fold creases along the top and bottom. b. Starting at the left side fold in the top perpendicular to the side and tightly fold over each triangular shaded area in turn. Do the same for the bottom, except that the bottom ends are folded flat while the top ends are perpendicular to the sides.

5. Rolling up the Vase. a. Roll up the left side, taking care not to change the valley and mountain folds. The end panels are overlapped, with the left side fitting on the outside of the right side. b. Push in the bottom folded edge against the inside of the vase to form the grooves to hold the stems. c. To make the top flat push up the pleats on top from the bottom, using a ruler. d. Hook the loose flap on top into the groove beneath.

Base for the Square Vase

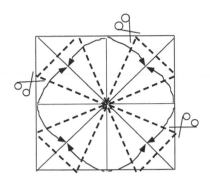

1. To make an octagon use 5 inch square paper to make a template. First crease diagonally and horizontally and vertically in half. Fold horizontal and vertical creases to the diagonal ones. Cut off at the ends of creases to get an octagon. Use it to cut an octagon on a 5 inch square posterboard covered with foil paper.

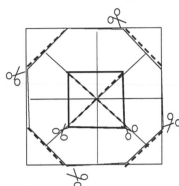

2. Center the square hole of the vase on the base with four sides parallel to the sides of the base. Then trace the outline of the vase onto the poster board. Using a razor knife cut through the diagonals of the inner square along the inside of the square.

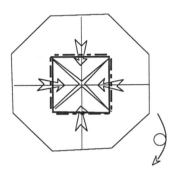

3. Score the outline of the vase and push in the four flaps to the foil side. Then turn to the foil side.

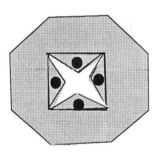

4. The Base for the Square Vase. Put some poster putty on the inner flaps and fit the vase surrounding the four flaps.

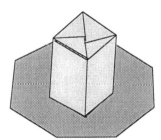

6. The Square Vase and Its Base. They need not be the same color.

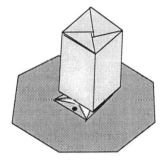

5. Press the triangular flaps firmly from the inside to stick the poster putty to the inside of the vase.

Base for the Hexagon Vase

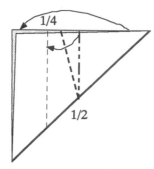

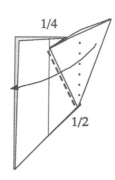

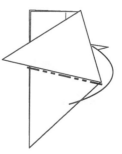

1. To cut a hexagon for the hexagon base, use the same size paper to cut a template. First fold the sheet along the diagonal and mountain fold the vertical 1/2 line and follow with a 1/4 marker. Then fold the end of the 1/2 line to the 1/4 line.

2. Fold over the right flap over along the crease line.

3. Mountain fold the lower half along the folded in edge. Three 60 degree angles are formed at the center of the sheet.

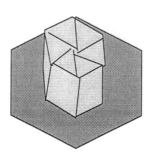

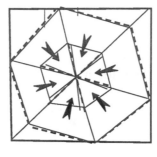

6. **The Hexagon Vase and Its Base.**

5. From this point on follow the instructions for the square vase. Complete the template, transfer its outline on the poster board covered with foil, cut the hexagon and the inner triangular flaps. Install this under the hexagon vase, with poster putty on the triangular flaps.

4. To get a hexagon cut from lower corner to the upper corner.

Chapter 10 FOLDING STEMS AND LEAVES

Stems

Experience with the first edition of the book indicated that the three sizes of stems were overall too weak when faced with fuller arrangements or stems which stretched out horizontally. Consequently base stems are being increased in size from 1/3 of 10 inches to 1/2 of 10. Middle stems are increased from 1/4 of 10 to 1/3 of 10 inches, while the end stems are increased from 1/6 to 1/4 of 10 inches.

One of the weakness of the opening of stems was that under pressure from inserted stems the hole was likely to open out. This was the result of the stem being started as a three sided tube with only a single side doubled up. Consequently a lesson learned from Andy Moul, a colleague at Brown University, the tube was built from the paper divided into eight parts, allowing for the wrapping of the tube more than two times around. This still retained the shape of the three-sided tube, which could be finished as before with a solid stem beyond the hole. There are also more precise instructions for folding the base, middle and end stems.

Leaves

The narrow and long leaves folded from a paper 1/6 of 10 inches and 5 inches long was used for all flowers, although it was originally developed for the wheat stalk. There was a need for rounder leaves for most flowers. For example, the rose has small leaves which are rounded at the stem end and pointed at the other end. There are other flowers with rounder leaves. Instructions have been added for smaller leaves folded from 2.5 inch square paper, which can be easily cut from 5 inch square paper. and easily folded without distinction between right and left sides. Also bulb flowers such as lily, tulip and daffodil have long leaves and non-branching stems, and instructions have been worked out for them.

Also included from the previous edition are a maple leaf, the wheat stalk, and a leaf based on the wheat stalk.

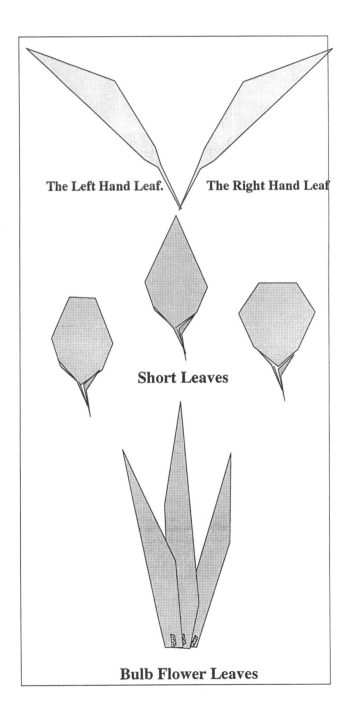

The Left Hand Leaf.   The Right Hand Leaf

Short Leaves

Bulb Flower Leaves

Cutting Paper for Stems and Leaves

1/2	6" Base	1/4	4" End
		1/4	End
1/2	5" Base		5" Spare

1/2	5.5 Base	1/2	4.5 Base
1/4	3" End	3" End	4" End
1/4	3" End	3" End	4" End

1/3	5" Middle	5" Middle
1/6	5" Leaf	5" Leaf
1/6	Leaf	Leaf
1/6	Leaf	Leaf
1/6	Leaf	Leaf

1. Take three heavy foil paper of the desired color for stems and leaves. Cut the first sheet into half (5 inches). The first half is cut into 6 and 4 inches and the second into two 5 inch lengths. The 4 inch piece can be used for a base stem or cut into two end stems. The second sheet is cut into half for two base stems and the second half is cut into 1/4 inch widths for four 3" and two 4" end stems.

2. The third sheet is cut first into thirds, for the middle stems. The rest is cut into 1/6 lengths for leaves. There are provisions for four base stems, two middle stems and eight end stems. There are also sheets for eight leaves. For small leaves cut two 5 inch squares into eight 2.5 inch squares. The cut sheets are sufficient for small to medium size arrangements with three to seven flowers.

Branches from Stems

Many Japanese flower arrangments call for branches of three different lengths, which I will refer to simply as Tall, Middle and Short Branches. In addition in the filling out process branches can be placed close to one another as support or to fill an empty space. Stems can also be added to form branches on existing ones. These branches are made up of connected Base (B), Middle (M) and End (E) stems.

Long Branch: B6 + M 5 + E4

Middle Branch: B5 + M4 + E3

Short Branch: B4.5 + E3

Extra Branch: B5.5 + E4

Preliminary Folding of the Stems

These adjustments bring the different width paper to a common starting position for folding. and to fix the size of the holes in the stems. To make a hole bigger the starting position can be widened.

Base Stem	Middle Stem	End Stem

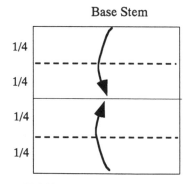

Fold both sides to the 1/2 line.

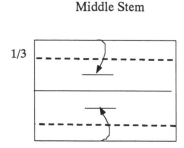

Fold in 1/3 of the way to the 1/2 line..

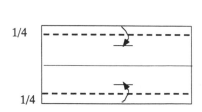

Fold in 1/4 of the distance to the 1/2 line.

Folding Base and Middle Stems

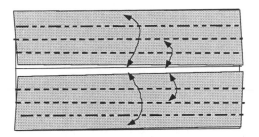

1. Divide into eights by folding both edges to the center twice and unfolding again.

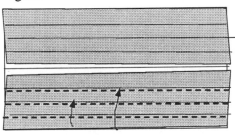

2. Fold over the lower edge to change the mountain fold to a valley fold. Then fold the edge over to the third line to form a triangle.

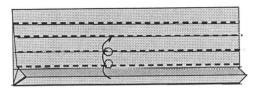

3. Roll the triangle over to the end as tightly as possible. This prevents the hole in the triangle from opening out when stems are pushed into it.

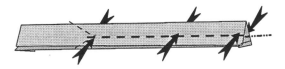

4. Place the piece on a flat surface and pinch both sides to form a T. Leave about an inch untouched at one end for a hole except for the end stem, which remains holeless.

Folding End Stems

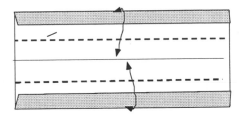

1. Fold edges to the center line and unfold.

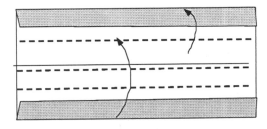

2. Fold the lower edge to the third line to form a triangular tube. Then go to Step 4 for the rest of the instructions.

5. The T Shape. Fold the two sides down by creasing down the center and pinching the two sides together. Again leave the hole section alone.

6. Fold the stem in half, except for the hole section.

Narrow Leaf Folding

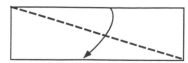

1. For a righthand leaf make a diagonal valley fold from the upper left to the lower right corner. Use a straight edge as a guide if necessary. To fold without it pinch the corners and form a rounded ridge before committing to a sharp edge.

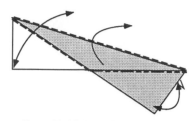

2. a. Fold the left corner against the raw edge of the folded down flap. Then open out again. b. Do the same for the right side. c. Open out the folded down flap along the diagonal line.

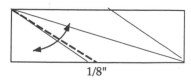

1/8"

3. On the left side fold a second line about 1/8" inside the first line. This second line will replace the first line.

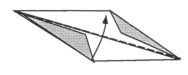

6. Fold in along the diagonal line.

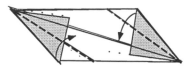

5. Fold in along the second line on the left and the single line on the right

4. To hide the excess paper at the ends, fold the lower left corner half way between the upper edge and the diagonal line. Repeat on the right edge

7. Fold in the small excess showing on the upper edge to hold in the open edge. Then use a rabbit-ear fold on the lower corner to form a stem.

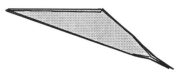

8. The underside of the right hand leaf. Flip over to the top side.

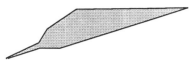

9. The top side of the right hand leaf.

The Left Hand Leaf

Either the right hand or left hand version of the leaf can be used for most situations, since both sides of the leaf are fairly well sealed.

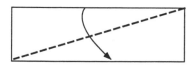

The Beginning of the Left Hand Leaf.

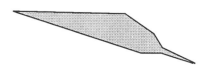

The top side of the left hand leaf.

Insertion of Leaves

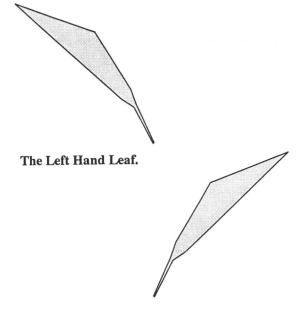

The Left Hand Leaf.

The Right Hand Leaf

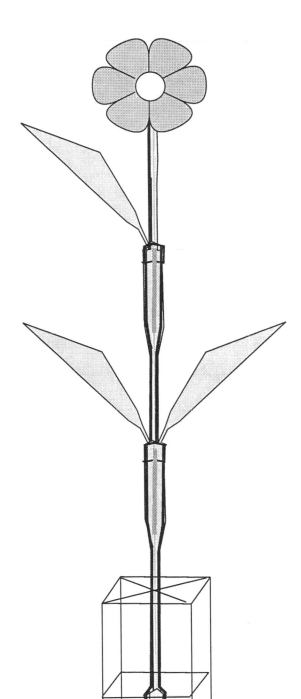

Left and Right Hand Leaves

The terms left hand and right hand arises from the fact that the long straight edge is folded and hence is best presented in front. The other edge can show some gap, but is generally not a serious problem.

Insertion of a Leaf

Use a sharp point of a pencil or round toothpick to make an opening at the hole, put a little bit of poster putty in the groove of the leaf stem, insert the leaf, press tightly from the outside to secure its position. Then shape the leaves as desired.

Function of the Leaf

Although leaves are a natural accompaniment of flowers, they can be removed if the arrangement is too fussy or full and added to cover gaps in the arrangement.

Leaves From a Kite Form

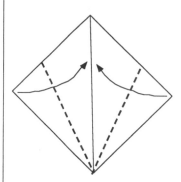

1. Start with a 2.5 x 2.5 inch paper with a vertical crease line in place. Fold sides to the center line to fold a kite form.

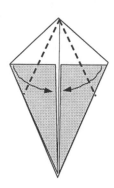

2. Fold the upper edges to the center line to fold a diamond shape.

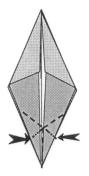

3. Use a rabbit ear fold to form a stem on about 1/3 of the bottom half. Sink the cross point and push in from the sides.

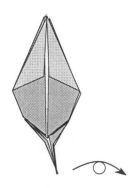

4. The underside of the leaf. Flip over.

8. **The Blunted Short Leaf.**

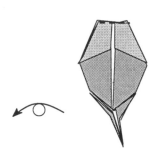

7. The underside. Flip over.

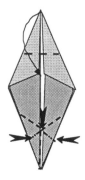

6. Start with the diamond fold and fold the top down to the crosspoint. Then use the rabbit ear fold to fold the stem.

5. **The Pointed Short Leaf.** Suitable for many flowers, including the rose.

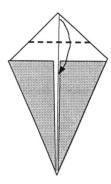

9. Start with the kite form. Fold down the top about 2/3 of the way down on the white area.

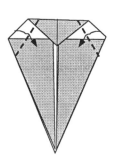

10. Fold in the right and left corners so that the three edges are about equal in width.

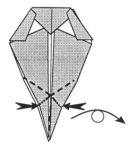

11. Use rabbit ear fold to shape the stem as before. Flip over.

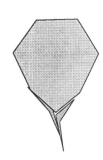

12. **The Roundish Leaf.**

Bulb Flower Stems and Leaves

Most flowers grow on branching stems to which flowers and leaves are attached. The stems and leaves of bulb flowers, such as iris, lily, tulip, daffodil, etc., grow directly out of the center of the bulb. The long stem for the flower grow straight up and usually supports a single flower at the end, while the leaves, which are also long and narrow grow straight up, surrounding the stem holding the flower. Thus the stem and leaves for bulb flower must be longer than for most flowers for which we have been dealing. and should be wrapped around the flower stem. Base stems are provided to hold each set of flower stems and leaves.

Cutting Stems and Leaves for Bulb Flowers

1/2	6" Base	4" Base
1/2	5" Base	5" Base

1/3	10" Tall Flower Stem
1/3	7.5 Middle Flower Stem
1/3	5" Short Stem 5" Short Stem

1/6	Leaf	10"
1/6	Leaf	9"
1/6	Leaf	8"
1/6	Leaf	8"
1/6	Leaf	7"
1/6	Leaf	6"

1/6	Leaf	6"
1/6	Leaf	5.5"
1/6	Leaf	5" 5" Leaf
1/2	Spare	

Tall Branch: B5 + M 10
+ Leaf 10
+ Leaf 9
+ Leaf 8

Middle Branch: B5 + M 7.5
+ Leaf 8
+Leaf 7
+ Leaf 6

Short Branch: B4 + M 5
+ Leaf 6
+ Leaf 5.5
+ Leaf 5

Folding Stems

Stems for the bulbs are folded as one would for end stems of other flowers.. The single long stem is begun like the middle stem, but is ended as one would an end stem--without a hole at one end, unless one chooses to put more than one flower at the end. Like the end stem it finishes up with folding into fourths instead of eights, folding a triangular tube and worked into a round stem.

Combining Stems and Leaves

Bulb leaves are generally wrapped around the single long stem and together are anchored in the hole of the base stem, which also helps to make the distinction among tall, middle and short branches. The use of a little poster putty is effective in keeping the leaves and stems together.

Folding the Bulb Leaves

1. Start with paper of the desired size. Use a straight edge and fold down along the diagonal line.

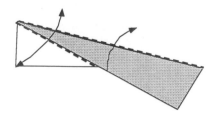

2. Fold the lower corner along the raw edge and unfold. I will refer to this as the first line. Then open out the upper half of the sheet along the diagonal line.

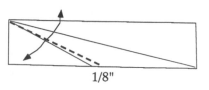

1/8"

3. Fold a second line above the first line ending in a width of about 1/8" along the lower edge (more if a narrower leaf is desired).

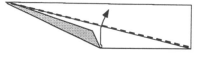

6. Fold along the diagonal line. The first line would have ended along the upper edge, but the second line leaves a little gap to help close the upper edge.

5. Fold over along the second line. The lower edge should not extend beyond the upper edge.

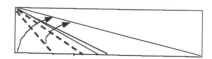

4. To reduce the amount of excess paper, fold the lower corner to the diagonal line , once or twice as needed, depending on the size of the paper. In our example, folding twice is necessary.

7. Fold down the upper righthand corner so that the upper edge just covers the raw edge of the lower fold (cover more if a narrower leaf is desired).

8. Fold in the narrow edge along the top to close the gap. Also fold up the lower right edge to narrow the stem of the leaf.

9. Fold in a narrow ridge along the top of the right half of the leaf to provide it with extra stength.

12. The bulb leaf ready for wrapping around the flower stem.

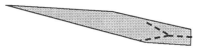

11. The upper side of the leaf. The bottom of the bulb leaf is usually wrapped around the central flower stem. However, if it is to be inserted by itself into a stem hole, narrow it down with a rabbit ear fold.

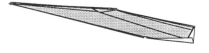

10. The underside of the bulb leaf.

Putting Bulb Leaves and Stems Together

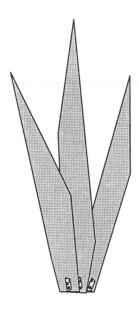

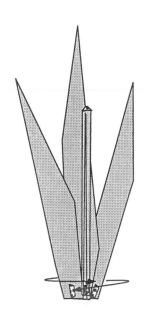

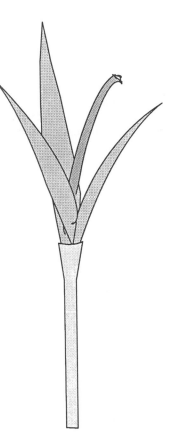

1. Take two or three leaves to be grouped together and put poster putty at the bottom. The tallest one should be in the middle with the smooth side up. Put the other two with one on each side in overlapped position, each one covering about 2/3 of the next one.

2. Place the single flower stem in the center. Then wrap the right side over the front. Then wrap the left side over it to keep the overlap in the same direction. Limit the wrapping to the bottom end of the leaves .

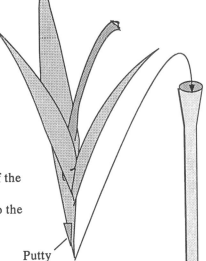

Putty

3. Take the wrapped end of the leaves and stem, add a little poster putty and insert it into the hole of the base stem.

4. The Completed Bulb Flower Stem and Leaf Combination. The leaves and the stem for the flower were arranged and bent outward to improve their appearance. A flower is attached to the top stem and the base stem goes into a vase.

The Maple Leaf

I made the maple leaf in 1969, according to my Origami Diary.
It can be used as a type of leaf for flowers.

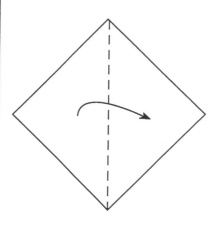

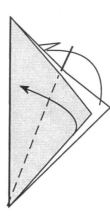

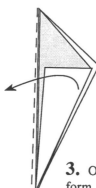

3. Open out into a kite form.

1. Start with a square sheet about three inches square with the uncolored side up. Make a diagonal fold.

2. Fold the lower side to the center line. Repeat behind.

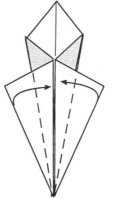

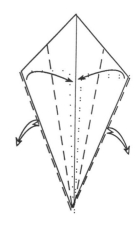

6. The narrow kite form. Fold the lower corners to the center line.

5. Fold in the sides to the center line.

4. Fold the folded edges on both sides to the center line. At the same time fold out the flaps hidden behind.

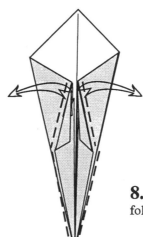

7. Fold the corners to the center line a second time.

8. Undo the preliminary folds.

The Maple Leaf--2

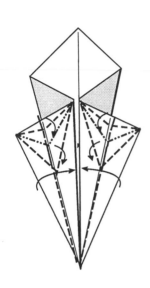 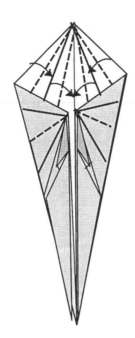 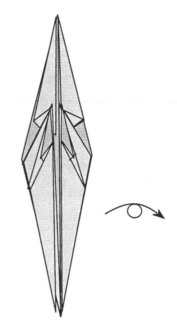 

9. Make corners with points by using V shaped accordion pleats. Start with the innermost valley fold. Then mountain fold and then valley fold. For the outer corner the preliminary creases will be off so fold to the corners.

10. Repeat Steps 6 to 9 on the upper corners, making preliminary creases and then doing accordion folds. This procedure produces two extra points and the base can be used to make a dinosaur.

11. Flip over to the underside.

12. Inside reverse fold the stem end of the maple leaf.

 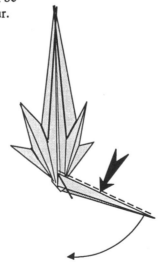 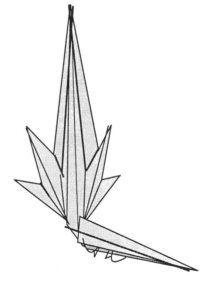

14. Move the stem into position by using an inside reverse fold. Push down on the folded edge and change the mountain fold to a valley fold.

13. Narrow the stem end by folding under.

15. **The Maple Leaf.**

The Wheat Stalk

The wheat stalk was developed a few years ago when I experimented with folding knots in a strip of paper. In 1991 when I developed the tube vase, it was the wheat stalk that I first used for arrangement before shifting to the use of flowers. The narrow leaf was developed then to go with the wheat stalks.

1. Start with a 10 inch strip of gold foil paper, cut to 1/6th of the width (about 1.7 inches). It can be a little wider. Crease in half and then fold both sides to the center line.

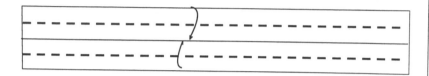

2. Mountain fold about four inches from the end and make a 60 degree bend by placing the lower corner on the center line.

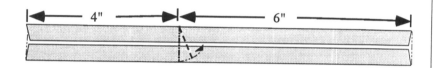

3. Valley fold in half the shorter stem end and then valley fold in half the longer section. This will produce a bend which is sometimes called a crimp fold. I have called it a foot fold, since it is often used for that purpose.

4. To make equally spaced diagonal mountain folds, fold the first fold upward toward the back and the second sideways toward the front. The effect is to wrap the strip around itself.

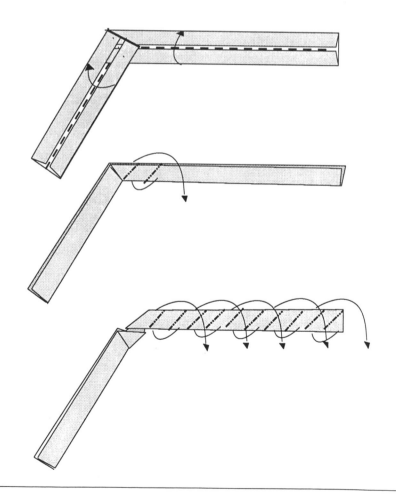

5. Continue the wrapping routine to the end. Then unwrap all of the folds.

The Wheat Stalk--2

6. Accordion pleat the wheat section by placing the second mountain fold on the first, the third on the second, etc. Then unfold the strip with the mountain folded center line on top.

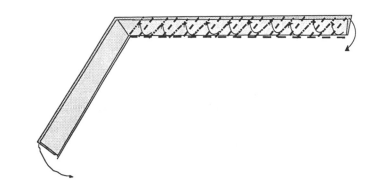

7. To make V shaped accordion pleats it is necessary to reverse the creases on the lower level. It will help to flatten out those creases first. Then fold the first V shaped mountain fold, follow it with a V shaped valley fold, and alternate in this manner to the end.

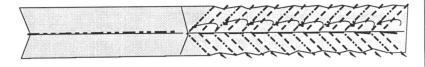

8. Narrow the stem end by mountain folding both sides to the center line.

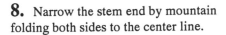

9. Narrow the stem end a second time, and squeeze the sides into a roundish shape. Spread out the middle of the wheat section, and press together the end. It is possible to form a curve to show a drooping stance.

10. **The Wheat Stalk.** The stem end can be inserted into the opening of a stem and a leaf added.

The Accordion Pleated Leaf

1. Start with a 5 inch strip of stem paper (3.3 inch wide) or half of a five or six inch square paper. Use one quarter for the stem and fold as one would the wheat stalk. At the end spread out the leaf and fold in the underside of the tip so that the two sides are held together.

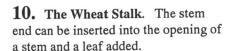
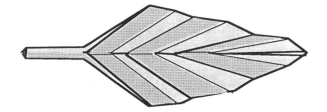

Chapter 11 ARRANGING ORIGAMI FLOWERS

Introduction

Japanese flower arrangement or *Ikebana* has a long history with some changes over time. There are many schools of flower arrangement and the three most popular ones are *Ikenobo*, *Sogetsu* and *Ohara*.. Some old styles of arranging flowers, such as *Rikka,* have given way to the less formal *Nageire* and *Moribana*. *Nageire* uses a tall vase and *Moribana* employs a flat one. In spite of these variations Japanese flower arrangement has some distinctive features. The most outstanding one is its attempt to depict plants and flowers as growing in its natural state. It shares this feature with Japanese gardens, which avoid geometric symmetry and strive for a natural appearance. Parts of plants, such as flowers, stems and leaves generally do not like to be bunched up together, but naturally spread themselves out within the limits of the space. Thus Japanese flower arrangement stresses simple natural looking forms rather than the bunched up appearance emphasizing the colorful mass.

The origami flowers, the stems and leaves are far from realistic, and one might question the audacity of attempting to emulate the arranging of real flowers. Fortunately, attempt at a natural appearance does not mean copying nature exactly. It only needs to appear natural. In addition the arranger can impose his own idea of what he considers to be attractive. To quote a Japanese encyclopedia article the truth is not necessarily the truth, and the false is not necessarily false.

A question can be raised as to whether it is possible to teach the achievement of natural appearance. As a matter fact, however, beginning books on flower arrangement are very specific about how to go about making an arrangement, at least at the elementary level. Added to this is the fact that using origami, it is possible to control all of the elements such as the size and color of flowers, the length of stem segments and their combined lengths, and the size and placement of leaves. Hence it is not necessary to deal with the dead leaves, the inconvenient branch, stems that refuse to bend or remain in position, etc. These introduce the need for dealing or handling the plants in a way which is not always easy to explain.

Three Main Stems

It is probably not an exaggeration to say that the foundation of Japanese flower arrangement rests on starting out with three main stems of different sizes, which I shall refer to simply as tall, medium and short, rather than their Japanese designations: *Shin, Soe, Hikae* or *Tai*. Since the arrangements of these can be limited, the task of arranging flowers can be viewed as approachable. Additional branches often need to be added, but it is possible to keep these somewhat limited. In origami flower arrangement it is possible to add leaves and flowers to connections in the stems, and this permits us to stick pretty much to the notion of dealing primarily with three different main stems.

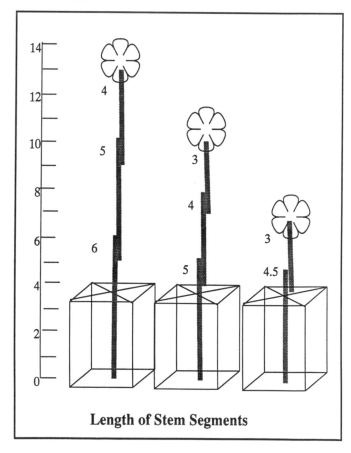

Length of Stem Segments

The lengths to which the stems are cut are related to the size of the vase, and a formula is available to accomplish this. The size of the vase can be measured by adding its height and width. Our vase is roughly 3.5 inch high and 2.5 inch wide, so that its size is 6 inches. The height of the tallest stem should be at least 1.5 times the height of the vase or 9 inches or more. At 2 times the height of the vase it would be 12 inches. At 2.5 times the height it would be 15 inches, which is probably about the outer limit of an ordinary arrangement. The middle stem should be about 3/4 of the tall one and the short one 3/4 of the middle one. Keeping these rules in mind and trying out different combinations, I have selected the stems to be made up of the following segments:

Tall: 6 + 5 + 4 = 15
Middle: 5 + 4 + 3 = 12
Short: 4.5 + 3   = 7.5 inches

About an inch will be lost when one stem segment is inserted into another. On the other hand, adding the flower at the end will increase the total

The Single Long Stem

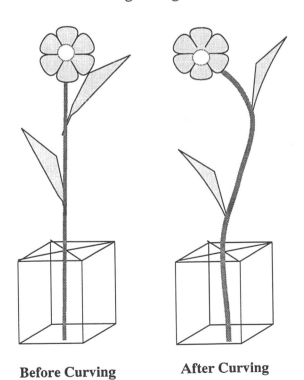

Before Curving   **After Curving**

length of a flower stem. It is desirable that the segments be located at different levels, since this provides for leaves to start and end at different levels--again in the interest of maintaining a natural appearance. Thus the ability to control the lengths of the stem segments adds to the ease with which an arrangement is completed. For example, the base stems are fixed at 6 for the tall, 5 for the middle and 4.5 for the short stem. Leaves inserted into these stems will start and end at different levels, providing the difference in levels of elements which is considered desirable.

The Single Long Stem

It is not unusual to see a single stem of flower displayed in a Japanese home and it often has an attractive shape. Understanding of the natural tendencies of plant segments to move away from one another provides the graceful form of growing plants. We first connect the stem segments to provide a single long stem. At the end a flower is placed, by inserting the end of the end stem into the bottom hole provided in the flower. Next a leaf is inserted into the first node. The flower and the leaf should be made to veer away from one another, causing a curve in the stem. A second leaf is placed in the node below, but not exactly opposite the first leaf. Fortunately, the stem is triangular in shape and it is possible for the flower and the two leaves to form a triangle. Again the leaf and the stem are curved to move away from one another, thus producing a second curve in the stem. The exact positioning of the leaves will depend upon the needs of the total arrangement. Some flower stems grow more or less straight because they have opposing pairs of leaves, but the curving stem with a single leaf at each node is to be preferred to achieve the natural and graceful appearance. This single stem can be placed in a vertical, slanting or horizontal position. In making arrangements one of the goals to keep in mind is the effective display of the curved stems-- particularly the longest one. For origami flower arrangement this is an outstanding feature because the stem is free of obstructions found in real plants.

The Asymmetrical Triangle

In the instructional section of *Ikebana* books there is a formula of sorts to guide the placement of the three stems of unequal lengths for the more modern *Nageire* and *Moribana*. To maintain the natural appearance it is desirable to place

Nine Basic Positions

Upright

Slanting

Horizontal

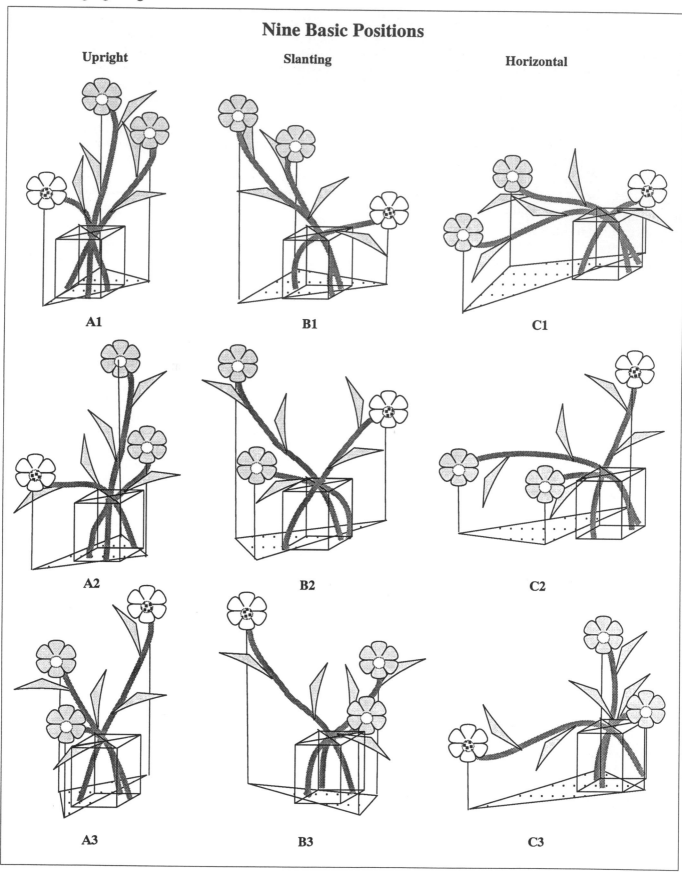

A1

B1

C1

A2

B2

C2

A3

B3

C3

them in a triangular arrangement, with two of them closer to one another than the other--i.e. to form an asymmetrical triangle. Perfect balance with one in the center and two equidistant from it is not desirable. Furthermore the triangular arrangement should hold when viewed from the top as well as from the front. This means that at least one leg of the triangle should be in front or back of the vase. When viewed from the front the flowers at the end of the stems should end at different levels.

When Mrs. Yasko Suzuki originally arranged the three wheat stalks for me for the Black Ship festival in Newport, Rhode Island, she had two of the wheat stalks close together drooped together in a similar way, while the other one faced in the opposite direction. I have adopted this as a way of organizing the relationships among the three stems. Two of the stems which are closer together can be viewed as growing up in a similar way. They can be reaching out in the same direction as though reaching for the light or being blown by the wind, for example. The one standing alone can stand in contrast. It can be growing away from the pair in a different direction and possibly different manner. This scheme provides a means of arranging similarities and differences, both of which are desirable for artistic effect. There are, of course, many other possible ways of conceptualizing an arrangement.

The asymmetrical triangle assures that the resulting structure is not fully balanced. There is more weight on one side of the vase than the other. The third stem can be seen as a counteracting element, sometimes stretched out in the opposite direction to provide some balance. Perfect balance, however, is not desirable, and it is proper for the arrangement of three stems to be leaning in one direction or another. The degree of imbalance can be varied by placing the stems closer together and reducing the degree of asymmetry or by adding counterbalancing items.

Positions

There are three general positions for stems-- upright, slanting and horizontal. If straight up is 0 degrees, then slanting can be considered at 45 degrees and horizontal at 90 degrees. Variations of up to 30 degrees in either direction are possible in actual working situations. It is easiest to fix the position of the longest stem first as upright, slanting or horizontal. Then it can be paired with the middle or the shortest stem or stand by itself. This provides nine basic combinations as a starter. In

combining two stems to work closely together it is possible to place the second one in front or behind the other. This makes a difference in appearance as well as the triangular arrangement that is suitable. Also, in pairing two stems their positions can be interchanged. A stem on top can be placed on the bottom or if it is to the right, it can be placed on the left of the other one with which it is paired. While there are basically nine positions outlined here, each of these can be varied in four different ways, excluding the possibility of flipping the whole arrangement from the left to the right side.

On Page 76 are shown the nine basic stem positions. The positions in which the long stem is vertical are labeled A1, A2, and A3. Where the long stem is slanting the labels are B1, B2 and B3. When the long stem is horizontal the positions are labeled C1, C2, C3. These are my own designations for convenience in identifying a selected position. In A1, B1, and C1 the long stem is paired with the middle size stem. In A2, B2 and C2 the long stem is paired with the short stem. There is usually a gap between the long and middle stems which need to be filled. In the A3, B3 and C3 situations, the long stem stands apart from the other two, which are placed closer together. By following these set patterns it should be possible to take the first step toward arranging the flowers Japanese style.

Insertion of Stems into the Vase

The vase should be faced so that the side with the overlapping panels is in the back. After the stems are put together in three sizes and a position has been selected, the stems can be curved into the shape indicated by the diagram. A little poster putty should be placed in the groove of the end of the base stem before insertion into the groove at the bottom of the vase. The base stem should be kept as straight as possible to retain its strength. A stem is inserted in the center opening of the closed end of the vase, but it can also be inserted along the diagonal slits, but the opening slants only in one direction. Inserting the end of the stem into the groove can be guided by one hand reaching into the vase from the underside opening and the bottom of the vase squeezed to strengthen the hold of the poster putty. In the diagram the vertical lines and the triangle connecting them indicate the rough location of the top of the stem as it is projected down to the level of the bottom of the vase. The triangle will indicate whether the stem should be to one side, in front or behind the vase. It should not be difficult to hold the three stems in place since they are held in position by the groove at the bottom and the small opening at the top of the vase.

Attaching the Flower.

Before attaching the flowers to the end of the stems, it is desirable to have some idea of the direction or attitude of the stems. Are the flowers to reach straight up, reach out sideways or droop their heads. Since Japanese flower arrangements are generally viewed from one side primarily, the flowers should at least face partially to the front where they can be seen easily. The two stems which are paired together should generally be given the same attitude or stance and be prepared first. The flowers for them, which should be similar in appearance, except perhaps for size, can be attached to the ends of the stems by insertion into a hole or in the case of some flowers into a slit. A little poster putty put in the groove at the end of the stem can help to keep the flower from falling off, particularly when being transported.

The third stem serves as a counterbalance to the first two and its distance from the other two stems and its angle of incline should be determined with this in mind Also, the flowers for the third stem group can be of a different color, size or variety, faced in the opposite direction, have a different attitude (for example, drooping when the other two are lifting their heads). The general aim is to maintain a harmony between balance and tension.

Adding Leaves

Leaves are generally folded the same color as the stems. If one is knowledgeable about flowers leaves can be matched with flowers, but otherwise the standard long or short leaves provided here can be used. Poster putty is placed inside the groove of the stem end of the leaf. In positioning a leaf, one should consider the position of the flower. Generally, the leaf should face away from the flower. The stem hole is triangular and the end stem and two leaves can form a triangular relationship. Leaves are also expected to help fill the gaps between the three main stems, and they often can be placed to fill that function. This may determine where and how the leaf is best placed-- It can reach straight up or out, it can be curved as though affected by the wind, or it can droop down as flowers can. The long narrow leaves are

particularly effective for this purpose.

Additional Flowers

Three stems and flowers, accompanied by appropriately positioned leaves can stand alone as a simple arrangement. In Japanese flower arrangement additional stems with flowers or leaves are often added to the basic arrangement of the three main stems. These supporting stems are generally shorter than the stems they support. In our arrangement it is possible to add a short stem and a flower directly to the stem itself. For the main and middle stems a flower can be added to one or two nodes , which may already have one or two leaves. This addition can be made on the same side as the leaf or on the opposite side, depending on where the gap needs to be filled. In A2+, B2+ and C2+ are shown the basic arrangement augmented by the addition of a flower to the long and middle stems. Clearly they help to fill gaps between stems and fill out the arrangement. The short stem can also be made to take two or three different stems of different lengths and a flower added to each. When the short stem is the odd one made up of a flower of contrasting color, a favorite arrangement is to increase this to two or three flowers, which helps to anchor the arrangement and also provide a contrasting focal point.

Additional Supporting Elements

Thus far we have maintained the notion of three main stems arranged in an asymmetrical triangle to achieve the natural appearance. Addi-

A2+

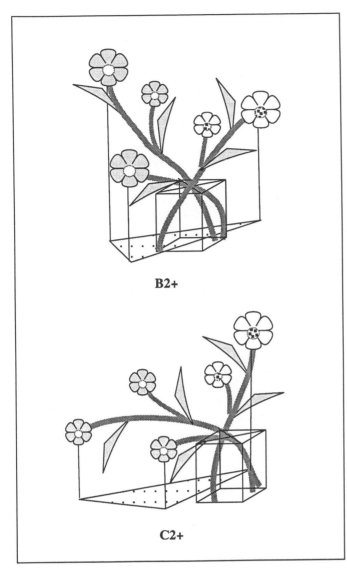

B2+

C2+

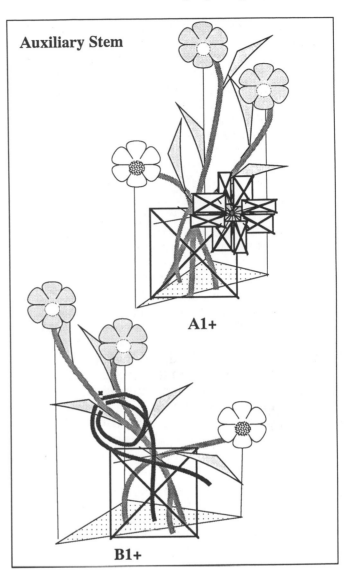

Auxiliary Stem

A1+

B1+

tional supporting stems can be used to improve the three stem arrangement. If there is an empty space in the back, the auxiliary element can be placed there, although it may not be too visible from the front. The most likely position for this auxiliary stem is in front on top of the vase, particularly if this area appears empty. There it can help to anchor the entire arrangement or provide for a needed contrast. I have tried a large silver flower for this role. This contrasting element might take a completely different form. One that I have used is the twisting vine, which can be constructed from a long thin stem and made to curl around a stem. Wheat stalks can be combined with flowers to provide some contrast. The traditional water bomb or balloon can be folded in copper to simulate the Chinese lantern. Dry flowers of all kind can be arranged in the vase,

but can also be combined with origami flowers. It is possible to have an auxiliary element both in front and the back, bringing the basic count of flowers to five.

Centerpiece Treatment

Supporting stems are often needed in the back of the arrangement, either because there is an empty space that calls for filling or because the arrangement is intended for a table centerpiece to be viewed from all sides. The fourth supporting element can be placed in the back rather than the front or one placed in the front as well as the back.

Another possibility is to add a stem to the back as a part of a second triangle designed to be viewed from the back. This will result in a different pairing arrangement in the back than exists in the front. In C2+ a short stem has been added to the back, and the back view shows that it has been paired with the upright stem. See also Photos 9, 10, 11 and 12 for treatment possibly suitable for a centerpiece. Some flowers, such as the bell flower or the lily, as well as the wheat stalk, are more suitable than others for viewing from all sides. Also, it helps to have additional flowers on the main stems, since some of them can be faced to the back.

Sample Arrangements

Japanese generally prefer odd numbers to even ones, but this should not deter an arranger from using four or six flowers, if it seems right. On the following pages are three sets of photographs of arrangements. These were taken from the front, but from a high position, in order to bring out the triangular arrangement as seen from the top. The first set (Photos 1-4) consists of simple arrangements of the basic three stems, with the possible addition of an additional supporting element in the front or back. The second set (Photos 5-8) are basically arrangements of five flowers. The last set (Photos 9 - 12) are made up of the full complement of seven flowers, with two flowers added to stems and two extra added in front and the back. These are the most likely candidates for a centerpiece.

Other Possibilities.

There are many other possibilities beyond what was attempted here--simple Japanese style flower arrangement forms applied to flowers, stems and leaves folded by origami techniques. Each folder flower arranger is free to conceptualize his own idea of what constitutes an ideal flower arrangement. One can concentrate on the four seasons, types of flowers and their particular habits, moods suitable for a happy or somber occasion, wild ideas calculated to get people's attention. All rules set forth here are simply guide lines to get started, and they can be broken. In the final analysis, one must judge for oneself what looks attractive or look to the judgement of others.

In 1983 Joan Appel and Alice Gray published a booklet titled **Origami Flowers and flower arrangement.** It contained a small collection of origami flowers which were not too difficult to fold, and relied on wires, tapes and glue to put the stems, leaves and flowers together. It also included a bowl in which to place the arrange-

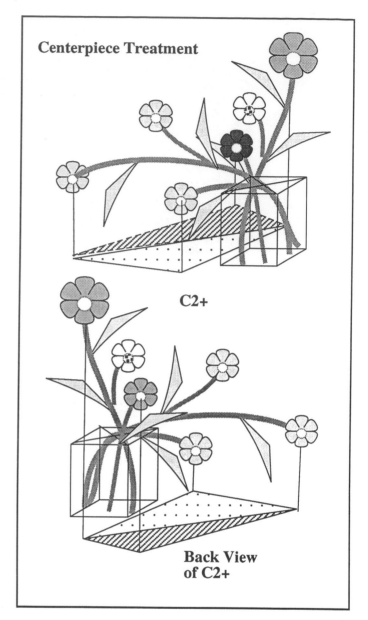

Centerpiece Treatment

C2+

Back View of C2+

ment. It represented the record of a two-session workshop given by the Friends of the Origami Center of America. It is hoped that more workshops will be held around the world to provide people, folders and non-folders alike, with knowledge and skill to produce works that will fulfill their creative needs.

1

2

3

4

5

6

7

8

9

10

11

12